GEISEL LIBRARY
LA JOLLA, CALIF

PLANNING, PEOPLE AND PREFERENCES

For Julie

and for Megan and Liam

Planning, People and Preferences

A Role for Contingent Valuation

RICHARD K O'DOHERTY

Avebury
Aldershot • Brookfield USA • Hong Kong • Singapore • Sydney

© R. K. O'Doherty 1996

All rights reserved. No part of this publication may be reproduced, stored in a retrieval system, or transmitted in any form or by any means, electronic, mechanical, photocopying, recording or otherwise without the prior permission of the publisher.

Published by
Avebury
Ashgate Publishing Limited
Gower House
Croft Road
Aldershot
Hants GU11 3HR
England

Ashgate Publishing Company
Old Post Road
Brookfield
Vermont 05036
USA

British Library Cataloguing in Publication Data

O'Doherty, R. K.
    Planning, people and preferences : a role for contingent valuation
    1. Planning - Citizen participation
    I. Title
    711.4 ' 0941

ISBN 1 85972 176 1

Library of Congress Catalog Card Number: 96-85552

Printed in Great Britain by The Ipswich Book Company, Suffolk

Contents

List of tables   viii
List of figures   ix
Acknowledgements   xi
Preface   xiii

Chapter 1   Introduction   1

   1.0   A Rationale and Justification   1
   1.1   Revealed Preferences: From Arrow to Aggregation   2
   1.2   Passive versus Active Participation   9
   1.3   Overall Aims and Objectives   13

Chapter 2   Public Participation in Developing Local Plans   17

   2.0   Introduction   17
   2.1   The Evolution of Planning Models   18
   2.2   Recent Developments in Public Participation   21
   2.3   Public Participation - Some Current Practices   25
   2.4   A Rationale for the Use of Contingent Valuation
          in the Participatory Process   31

| Chapter 3 | Cost-effective Preference Revelation | 35 |

3.0	Introduction	35
3.1	Total Economic Value - Categories of Benefits	36
3.2	Indirect Valuation Techniques	43
3.3	The Contingent Valuation Method - An Overview	46
3.4	Measuring Consumer's Surplus	47
3.5	Error and CVM - Issues of Validity and Reliability	54
	3.5.1 Validity	56
	3.5.2 Reliability	63
3.6	Benefit Transfer - An Overview	66
	3.6.1 The Demand for Benefit Transfers	67
	3.6.2 Approaches to Benefit Transfer	79
	3.6.3 A Summary of Benefit Transfer	74
3.7	Sources of Error in CVM Surveys	76
	3.7.1 Respondent-Based Sources of Error	77
	3.7.2 Researcher-Based Sources of Error	82
3.8	A Guide to Good Practice	88
3.9	Summary and Conclusions	93

| Chapter 4 | Factorial Survey Design | 95 |

4.0	Introduction	95
4.1	Modelling Individual Choice	96
4.2	Factorial Surveys: Design and Analysis	98
4.3	Linking Factorial Survey Design and the Contingent Valuation Method	99

| Chapter 5 | Enhancing Public Participation | 103 |

5.0	Introduction	103
5.1	The Bristol North Fringe Local Plan	103
5.2	Objectives of the Empirical Work	104
5.3	Design of the Application	105
5.4	Data Analysis and Interpretation of Results: Surveys 1 and 2	111
	5.4.1 The Respondents' Experience	131
5.5	Conclusion and Shortcomings	132

Chapter 6		Summary and Conclusions	135
	6.0	Introduction	135
	6.1	Public Participation - Current Practice	135
	6.2	Potential Improvements	137
	6.3	Principal Findings from the Fieldwork	140
	6.4	Concluding Remarks	142

Appendices 143

Appendix 1 Questionnaire: Public Participation/Consultation at District Level 143
Appendix 2 Background Information and Questionnaire 149
Appendix 3 Questionnaire: Additional Questions 156

Bibliography 159
Index 175

List of tables

2.1	Informing the General Public	26
2.2	Presenting Plans to the General Public	28
2.3	Receiving Responses from the General Public	29
2.4	Gauging Intensity of Feeling	29
2.5	The Degree of Importance Attached to Preferences of the General Public	39
3.1	Willingness to Pay for Selected Classes of Goods and Allocations of Totals to Less Inclusive Groups	41
3.2	Behaviour-based Methods of Valuing Public Goods	44
3.3	Comparisons between Direct and Indirect Valuations of a 50% Change in Perceived Pollution Levels	62
3.4	Net Economic Values per Recreation Day Reported by Travel Cost and Contingent Valuation Demand Studies from 1968 to 1988, United States (third quarter 1987 dollars)	71
3.5	*A Priori* Expectations of Strategic Behaviour in CV Settings	78
3.6	Potential Sources of Information Related Bias in CVM Surveys	85
3.7	Methodological Requirements for CVM Surveys of Recreation Value	89
3.8	AMA and MRS Focus on Subject's Rights in Market Research	92
5.1	Frequencies: Surveys 1 and 2	118
5.2	Simple Correlations: Surveys 1 and 2	122
5.3	Regression Results: Surveys 1 and 2	124

List of figures

2.1	The Geddesian Model	18
2.2	Simon's Decision Model	19
2.3	Choice Theory	20
2.4	Eight Rungs on a Ladder of Citizen Participation	22
3.1	Compensating Measures of Welfare Gain and Loss for an Unpriced Quantity Constrained Environmental Good	48
3.2	Varying the Marginal Rate of Substitution	49
3.3	Where X is an Inferior Good	49
3.4	The Case of a Unique or Irreplaceable Environmental Good	49
3.5	Asymmetrical Total Value Curve Showing WTP/WTA Variation	53
3.6	Validity	55
3.7	Reliability	55
3.8	Fishbein-Ajzen Model for Predicting Specific Intentions	58
3.9	Continuum of Decision Settings from Least Required Accuracy to Most Required Accuracy	68
3.10	Continuum of Validation Scrutiny in an NRDA Context	69
3.11	Likely Recommended Use of BT: By Researcher's Optimism and Required Accuracy	69
3.12	The Relationship between Theoretical and Methodological Mis-specification	84
4.1	A Model of Individual Choice	96
4.2	Litchfield's Community Impact-Analysis Procedure	97
5.1	Survey 1	114
5.2	Survey 2	117
5.3	Averages: Surveys 1 and 2	130

Acknowledgements

I am indebted to the many people who have read extracts of this work and who have provided helpful comment. My thanks go first of all to Professor David Pearce, who has a knowledge of the range of relevant literature and access to pertinent networks which is second to none. His guidance throughout has been a valued asset. I must also mention various colleagues at my institution, University of the West of England, Bristol, especially Tony Flegg, who has, for too many years, suffered a relentless barrage of questions and demands for his time. Thanks are also due to Nick Oatley, who gave advice and direction to the early stages of the work, and to Chris Webber and Peter Taylor for their advice on the appropriate analysis of the survey data. I am grateful also for the considerable improvements to the work resulting from initial readings by Professor Lord Desai and Professor Ken Willis.

As there have been various publications resulting from the work as it progressed (see preface), thanks are also due to numerous anonymous referees. Furthermore, whilst students, seminar participants and conference delegates may not recognize their individual influences, it is only fair to state that their comments have helped to shape the work.

With regard to the more practical aspects, I express my thanks to Christine Hunt and her colleagues, who provided accurate and speedy secretarial support.

Finally, I would like to thank the Centre for Social and Economic Research (CESER) in the Faculty of Economics and Social Science, UWE, for its continued support throughout the project.

Preface

The initial intention was merely to satisfy a personal curiosity. Having been dismayed at the lack of useful public participation processes in my locality, I began by questioning by whom, where, when and how planning decisions were taken. My first excursion was to view the relevant process in action in South Bristol, held at an outreach office of the Council's Housing department. Obviously appearing other than as a potentially interested party at the planning exhibition, I was told that the Housing Office was closed. I enquired after the planning exhibition and was met with stunned disbelief. I had been one of very few people to visit the exhibition on that day, and the sole member of staff was already preparing to close shop. Whilst the work reported here does not address all the problems associated with public participation in planning decisions, or all the potential solutions, it is hoped that it will stimulate further discussion on the empowering of local people.

As the work progressed, it culminated in various publications and conference papers.

'Using Contingent Valuation to Enhance Public Participation in Local Planning', drawing on the findings of Chapter 2 along with an initial appraisal of those from Chapter 5, is forthcoming in *Regional Studies*, 30, (7) 1996. An initial draft of Sections 3.1 to 3.5 and 3.7 to 3.9 of Chapter 3, was published in full as, CSERGE Working Paper PA93-01 (UCL and UEA), and provided the basis for the articles 'In Defence of Valuing Environmental Amenities', *Futures*, 25, (4), May 1993, and 'Pricing Environmental Disasters: The Case of Exxon Valdez', *Economic Review*, 12, (1), September 1994. Chapter 3, Section 3.6, was published separately as 'A Review of Benefit Transfer: Why and How?', in the *British Review of Economic Issues*, 17, (43), 1995.

Conference papers emanating from the work include; 'The Contingent Valuation Method', presented at the Values and the Environment Conference at the University of Surrey, September 1993; 'Planning, People and Preferences', presented at the European Association of Environmental and Resource Economists (EAERE) (Dublin) Conference, June 1994; 'Contingent Valuation and Benefit Transfer: An Assessment in a Local Planning Context', to be presented at the Conference on Integrating Environmental Assessment and Socio-Economic Appraisal in the Development Process, University of Bradford, May 1996; and 'The Valuation of Green Space and an Assessment of the Potential for Benefit Transfer in a Local Planning Context', to be presented at the EAERE (Lisbon) Conference, June 1996.

1 Introduction

1.0 A Rationale and Justification

The rationale for this work stems from a personal belief that true public participation in public decision-making, whilst increasing the potential for short term conflict, is likely to lead in the longer term to a more harmonious situation. Watching a local environment change for the worse and having little or no say in such developments leads to disillusionment for local people. Subsequently, this may lead to further deterioration of the environment due to a feeling of alienation from the decision-making process and thus a lack of ownership of the shape of developments.

Arrow's impossibility theorem (Arrow, (1951)), which is detailed in the next section, suggests that it is impossible to develop a method which is perfectly suited to the task of capturing the preferences of the general public. His work was the result of numerous criticisms aimed at welfare economists due to their reliance on cardinal measures of utility and the making of interpersonal comparisons on this basis. Ironically, Arrow, as part of a team of eminent economists (Arrow *et al.* (1993)), provided support to compensation claims in the US courts based on a technique, the contingent valuation method, which is firmly grounded in welfare economics and relies on both cardinal, monetary-based, measures of utility and interpersonal comparisons. Given that those in public service must make decisions which in many cases have a positive affect on some and a negative impact on others, it would seem that even Arrow would offer imperfect help as an economist rather than suggesting a complete withdrawl.

In a similar vein, the approach adopted in this work, whilst continuing along the same imperfect road, does contribute to the on-going debate concerning public participation in public decision making.

1.1 Revealed Preferences: From Arrow to Aggregation

In 1951, Arrow introduced his general possibility theorem which has become better known due to its negative conclusions as the impossibility theorem. This signalled significant difficulty for those seeking public opinion using preference revelation mechanisms. Four and a half decades later, at a symposium on voting mechanisms, reported in the Journal of Economic Perspectives, the lead paper by Levin and Nalebuff (1995) concluded with the following sobering thought:

> ....that (we) might stop .... from looking for some perfect Holy Grail of a voting method that meets all needs: a voting system can't find a consensus when none exists. (p 24)

It appears that Arrow's contribution was built on solid foundations. Sen (1995) would tend to agree. In his review of attempts which have been made either to refute or to avoid the impossibility theorem, Sen is forced to conclude that none has been successful. Instead, Sen comes to terms with the problem by calling for a 'less rigid interpretation' of Arrow's requirements. However, by relaxing either of the two axioms or any of the five conditions of Arrow's theorem means that other relevant economic and ethical principles need to be considered.

Arrow's two axioms are 'connectivity' and 'transitivity'. The former states that any mechanism of preference revelation must produce a result, either indicating preference for, or indifference between, any two alternatives. Transitivity may be seen as consistency. If x is preferred to y which in turn is preferred to z, then x must be preferred to z.

His first condition is needed to illustrate the limiting case where only three alternatives are presented to individuals for ordering. Arrow's proof that in this limiting case no scheme exists which could result in a true social ordering can then be widened to the case where more than three alternatives are offered. The second condition states that if an individual's values change then this is shown in a non-negative relationship with the social value. The independence of irrelevant alternatives, the third condition, states that the ordering of any two alternatives is not influenced by the presence (or absence) of a third or subsequent alternative. In the review of the contingent valuation method in Chapter 3, this condition is likened to the problem of 'embedding'. This problem arises when the ordering within a set of goods affects the valuation of those goods. Conditions four and five relate to non-dictatorship; the former avoiding imposition of an outcome by someone outside of the society and the latter to non-dictatorship from within the society.

Mueller (1989) and Sen (1995) provide detailed evaluations of Arrow's impossibility theorem. The approach adopted by Mueller is to consider the implications of relaxing each axiom or condition in turn. Given that relaxing either the axiom of connectivity or transitivity would result in an incomplete system or one which could become infinitely cyclical respectively, it would appear that these must remain intact.

A relaxation of condition one limits the social decision process to elementary cases which Dasgupta and Pearce (1972) dismiss as 'of little interest to anyone'. Willis (1980) concurs with this view stating that without this condition the most difficult cases, where opinions conflict, would remain unresolved. It also seems reasonable that condition two must stand. If the preferences of a member of the society change then this should be reflected in a non-negative change in the social ordering. The conditions relating to dictatorship, conditions four and five, are eminently reasonable on ethical grounds if a democratic stance is preferred.

In reviewing condition three, it is worth considering the rationale for Arrow's work in this area. Arrow was responding to the challenge of developing a social welfare function which did not rely on using cardinal measures of utility and without the need for interpersonal comparisons. It is this rationale, arising from the critiques of early welfare economics, that led to Arrow's rigid axioms and conditions. When conditions two and three are considered together, it becomes clear that for Arrow, individual orderings mattered but preference intensities did not. Using simple examples, Dasgupta and Pearce (1972) and Sen (1995) show that intensity of preferences and interpersonal comparisons respectively, question the reasonableness of Arrow's restrictions. For Arrow, there could be no distinguishing between the following two cases. Firstly, in case 1, individual x just prefers a to b and individual y just prefers b to a. In case 2, again, x just prefers a to b but here, y much prefers b to a. Is it reasonable to simply portray these two cases in the same light?

Sen considers the case where there are three possible divisions of a given cake between two individuals. The splits are (99,1), (50,50) and (1,99). Quite simply, given the assumption of *homo economicus* we expect each party to prefer more of the cake to less. If we consider the pair of alternatives, (99,1) and (50,50) and regard the latter as a better outcome for society then we give priority to person 2 over person 1, and, most importantly, we have made an interpersonal comparison. Sen goes on to illustrate that under Arrow's assumption, abandonment of the concept of cardinality and interpersonal comparisons, there can be no argument in support of equal divisions of the cake. Even where it is considered that equal divisions may equate utilities, this would be a violation for Arrow as it uses interpersonal comparisons of ordinal utilities.

It seems that in virtually all aspects of life interpersonal comparisons are used. Why then was Arrow so driven by the critique of interpersonal comparisons that he developed the impossibility theorem? Firstly, according to Mueller (1989), measurement of cardinal utility was considered to be difficult and arbitrary. Secondly, any process which sought to use interpersonally comparable, cardinal utilities would be open to abuse. In fact, Arrow's view of the collective choice process was one dominated by information-gathering public officials in whose hands cardinal-based interpersonal utility comparisons would bring a great deal of discretionary power. In order to circumvent such potential abuses of power and bearing in mind the strong critiques of cardinality and interpersonal comparisons, Arrow formulated his impossibility theorem. However, this was not the only route which could have been taken by Arrow. Indeed, to some extent the impossibility theorem plays right into the hands of potential abusers of public position. If decisions have to be made which bring both positve and negative affects, then interpersonal comparisons will be made. If political theorists and economists wash their hands of involvement because it is 'impossible' to do correctly, the potential abusers face little opposition. Indeed, Levin and Nalebuff's (1995) wide-ranging review of thirteen different categories of voting mechanisms does not reveal any that would satisfy Arrow's axioms and conditions. Avoiding the potential abuse of discretionary power in the hands of public officials demands that cardinal utility information be derived directly from the public. As Mueller states, some voting mechanisms are capable of extracting such information although these methods, such as point voting, are vulnerable to strategic manipulation by respondents.

Willis (1980) discusses some of the attempts made by planners to capture intensity of feeling in public participation exercises. South Yorkshire County Council (1975) for example, used point votes to develop an indication of intensity of feeling towards various problems which might be addressed in their local plan. The questionnaire and an allocation of 100 points were sent to various local groups who were asked to distribute these points among the topics (problem areas) which the planners would then address. Allocating an equal number of points to each group essentially sidesteps the problem inherent in cost benefit studies, that willingness to pay (vote) for something is dependent to some extent on ability to pay. In cost benefit analysis, unless some form of weighting of responses takes place, the existing (unequal) distribution of income is taken to be optimal. However, using votes instead of money leads to other problems. First, in this example, planners and respondents would have no indication of the total spending requirement to fulfil the chosen policies and second, the process is likely to result in strategic behaviour by respondents as, unlike with money, there is no incentive to save points.

Willis also reviews an attempt by Tyne and Wear County Council (1976) to introduce a link between a respondent's priorities and their willingness to pay to achieve those ends. This exercise was essentially an example of a Borda Count voting system with a question relating to the overall level of public spending in the area. The main criticism here is that the ordinal ranking did not reveal a respondent's intensity of preference. Furthermore, the very general question about the level of overall public spending in the area was not sufficiently detailed to link actual willingness to pay to individual policy topics. According to Mueller (1989), the Borda method, like point voting, is subject to potential strategic behaviour by respondents.

Obtaining cardinal utility information for decision making purposes, without encountering strategic manipulation, is one of the strengths of the contingent valuation method. In Chapter 3 it will be shown how this method minimises strategic manipulation and how, by using a money-based cardinal scale, additional information with regard to the extent of public spending can also be realised.

The discussion so far in this section portrays an escape from Arrow's impossibility therorem by reverting to cardinal-based measures of preferences. In effect, this brings the discussion full circle as the critiques levelled at cardinality and interpersonal comparisons provided the rationale for Arrow's work in the first place. These critiques have not disappeared but the body of literature on this topic since Arrow's original work has usefully highlighted the dilemma faced by those seeking to elicit public preferences. Either a voting system such as the Borda method is used and one or more of Arrow's conditions are violated or a cardinal-based measure is adopted which encounters the problems of interpersonal comparisons and aggregation.

The problems of making interpersonal comparisons and the related issue of aggregation may be examined separately. In order to compare the change in utility between individuals consequent upon, say, some alteration in public policy, it is necessary to assume that cardinal measures can be used. Instead of preference ordering of different outcomes, what is sought is the intensity of preference for the different outcomes. Thus, instead of a respondent indicating a preference for state x over state y, the information gleaned using cardinal scales is the extent of preference for state x over y. The problem, of course, is not at this conceptual level but rather at the operational level. Whilst two individuals may have underlying equivalent preferences for some change, they may each express this intensity differently given that utility is not objectively measurable. Notwithstanding this last statement, attempts have been made to develop cardinal measures of utility. In conventional cost benefit analysis the cardinal measure is based on a monetary scale. Thus, in likening public goods to a private good market where pound votes are taken to represent intensity of preference for a particular product, cost benefit analysis estimates changes in utility levels among individuals by how much they do pay (or in some cases would pay) to secure the preferred outcome. A problem immediately arises in that the ability to purchase a good in either a private of public good market is, to some extent, determined by ability to pay.

Given that a pound has a different value to an individual depending on, amongst other things, the stock of pounds held, it would appear that adopting such a money-based cardinal measure is flawed. Making interpersonal comparisons on this basis would also seem to lack justification. However, where decisions have to be made in the area of public policy and in the absence of any other preference revelation mechanisms which would satisfy Arrow's axioms and conditions, much effort has been expended in refining the money-based cardinal measures. For instance, if a monetary scale is accepted as a useful basis for such comparisons, the underlying (unequal) distribution of incomes can be accounted for by weighting the pound votes of individuals according to the stock of votes held. Social objectives could also be incorporated in the weighting mechanism.

Conventional cost-benefit analysis uses an implicit unitary weighting for all parties affected by a proposal. In using unitary weights in the analysis, the conventional approach assumes that the existing distribution of income is optimal. Those who disagree with this assumption, the revisionists as they are termed by Mishan (1982), occupy one of two sub-schools of thought. Firstly, those such as Little and Mirlees (1974) advocate that the choice of weighting be determined in accordance with political objectives. Quite simply, if it is a political or social objective to redistribute income and wealth from rich to poor, then weightings assigned to poorer groups who will gain or suffer from some proposal are increased relative to those of the richer groups. The second sub-school of revisionists advocate the use of value sensitivity analysis (Nash, Pearce and Stanley (1975)). Here, rather than a single weight being used, multiple sets of weightings are assigned which generate several sets of results. In this way, the decision maker can see how the final result of the analysis is affected by the weighting factor. Mishan (1974; 1981; 1982) offers various criticisms of the revisionist stance. For example, he argues that redistributions of income should be undertaken using fiscal measures rather than via project implementation.

Even though consensus on the issue of weighting is still sought, the provision of information using value sensitivity analysis should be welcomed by decision makers. Furthermore, cost-benefit analysis enshrines the normative judgment that peoples' preferences should count in the decision-making process. Kweit and Kweit (1987) take this concept as far as suggesting that the public should be asked what they consider to be an appropriate discount rate to be used in public sector project appraisal. Likewise, it is theoretically plausible to ask the public to determine the appropriate weightings for use in the analysis.

Use of the contingent valuation method in cost-benefit analysis may help to overcome some aspects of the weighting problem discussed above. If weightings ought to reflect a societal view of the deservedness of various groups, a viewpoint inherent when politicians determine weightings (politicians being elected to act on behalf of society), then direct estimation of these weightings by asking the public should give similar results. Rather than determining weightings separately though, in contingent valuation studies the respondent may determine the deservedness of various groups affected by different plans before valuing these alternatives. If this was the case, society's weightings would be implicit in the valuations given. To go on and use additional non-unitary weightings on the results of a contingent valuation study would be to distort the true picture. It is unclear, however, which stance respondents are likely to adopt. It might be hoped that all individuals would consider the implications for others of their privately preferred option. Such consideration may even result in a different choice of policy, although this could not be assured. Hammond (1991) reviews some mechanisms which could, in theory, make the social outcome more probable although these are predominantly philosophical in nature and are unlikely to be used in practice. For instance, Harsanyi (1953, 1955) suggests that respondents should answer as though they have no knowledge about which member of society they will be after the decision is made. This is akin to Rawls's 'veil of ignorance' (Rawls (1971)) although he has suggested taking this idea even further, recommending that respondents, when confronted with uncertainty of outcome, should behave as if they were in the position of the person they would least like to be. It should be apparent that much of this discussion concerns the elicitation of preferred outcomes from individuals in isolation from one another. According to Jacobs (1996) this institution, one of isolated individuals who according to the above discussion may or may not exercise choice from a social stance, produces the wrong outcomes for society. He argues that the correct process should entail a deliberative searching for a group consensus which he terms 'citizenship'. This implies that individuals' preferences, attitudes and values are transformable rather than given.

Sen (1967) raised a similar issue to that discussed above in his discussion of appropriate discount rates for use in cost-benefit analysis. He argues that individuals would choose one discount rate when considering costs and benefits from a 'private' standpoint and a different, lower, rate from their 'public' standpoint. The latter, Sen argues, depends upon an individual's belief that many others will also invest in a 'public' project.

The relevance here is in determining which hat respondents wear when engaged in contingent valuation. The 'private' hat would necessitate politicians weighting results. On the other hand, if individuals wear their 'public' hat, weightings may already be included in the valuations given. Admittedly, even where compensation is made for varying levels of income, this still leaves the issue of the varying marginal utility of money between respondents to be tackled. Whilst all guidelines on the weighting issue are open to some criticism, conducting value sensitivity analysis (using various weightings in a 'what-if' format) may prove least contentious. Interestingly, and following from Jacobs comments discussed above, if it is found that respondents wear their private hat, the whole application of contingent valuation may have to be reconsidered.

In the context of political voting, Brennan and Buchanan (1984) conclude that voters may vote symbolically where they believe they have little chance of affecting an outcome. They suggest that similar behavioural patterns may exist in economic preference revelation exercises such as those undertaken using contingent valuation. Mitchell and Carson (1989) on the other hand have reinterpreted these findings and conclude that Brennan and Buchanan's study shows instead that people behave in a more public spirited manner in political markets than they do in private goods markets. This reinterpretation would tend to support the argument here, that the weighting issue may be of lesser significance when valuation is carried out using a direct technique such as contingent valuation rather than observed-indirect methods such as the travel cost approach. Where, for instance, the contingent valuation method is set up as a political market, a cardinally-based referendum, weightings may already be embedded in individual responses. This is unlikely to be the case with observed-indirect methods of valuation.

If it is accepted that a reasonable departure from the Arrow impossibility therorem is to revisit the issues of cardinal measures of utility, varying marginal levels of utility of money and unequal distributions of incomes (weighting), a further choice faces the decision maker. The refined money-based measures may be aggregated using either an additive or multiplicative functional form. In the former we simply add all the positive and negative changes in the utility of the individuals affected and consider the overall outcome. However, this method of aggregation could, in principle, see one person made much worse off in state y than in state x (even to the point of zero utility) and where many others receive marginal positive changes in utility, as an overall positive social outcome. The multiplicative form would protect individuals from such a situation, never allowing the utility of one or more members of the society to fall to zero. Clearly, the choice of functional form has serious implications for the society although protection of individual members need not be solely dependent on this factor. It is quite possible to constrain any negative change in individual utility as part of that society's constitution.

Having alluded to the principal issues surrounding the debate which has ensued especially since the publication of Arrow's work, the approach adopted in later parts of this work, like cost-benefit analysis, is unashamedly based on a cardinal measure of the intensity of individuals' preferences. Planning, the relevant context of public policy addressed here, has considered only on rare occasions such an approach to public participation. However, whilst recognising the potential criticisms of such a stance, those criticisms should be considered in the light of both Arrow's work, suggesting that there are no perfect alternatives, and the demands made by society for public sector decision-makers to make decisions in areas of conflict. Such a stance is not one which merely ignores the issue of interpersonal comparisons of utility. Indeed, as Hammond (1991) acknowledges, even the choice of a dictator requires that interpersonal comparisons of utility be made. It should not seem strange that cost-benefit analysis incorporates such comparisons but rather it is odd that there are those who deny that interpersonal comparisons of utility constantly need to be made. Recognising that interpersonal comparisons cannot be avoided ought to be seen in a positive light. Energy can then be spent on the task of making sure that the basis for these comparisons is transparent and open to criticism.

The resolution of conflict is often a difficult process. Cost-benefit analysis is a tool developed by economists to assist in this process. In using cardinal measures of intensity of preference for or against some proposal, along with interpersonal comparisons and difficult decisions concerning aggregation, cost-benefit analysis is not without problems. An interesting additional difficulty arises when the valuation aspect of cost-benefit analysis is to be used as a referendum mechanism. Whether people feel disenfranchised from the process, or owners of the resolution of conflict, is also important. In the next section this issue of the degree of conscious involvement of the general public in the decision-making process as informed by cost-benefit analysis is considered.

1.2 Passive versus Active Participation

Cost-benefit analysis was formally recognised in the UK around 1960 and in the USA some twenty-five years earlier. In the USA, for example, the 1936 Flood Control Act stipulated that projects should be evaluated in terms of costs and benefits and that a project be considered desirable if the benefits 'to whomsoever they may accrue' are in excess of the estimated costs.

Earlier references to the concepts of social costs and benefits can be found, for instance, Dupuit (1844), who first formulated the concept of consumer surplus which was later developed and analysed by Marshall (1920). However, it is the apparent need of government agencies to begin to estimate social costs and benefits in practice, and therefore the formal inclusion of such in the evaluation of projects, which is of interest here.

Why, one might ask, did representative democracies feel the need to formalise what surely their constituents previously thought was included in the informal, political process of project evaluation? It is not unreasonable to expect those charged with public responsibilities to act in the interest of society as a whole. However, a number of reasons why this might not be the case can be hypothesised. First, constituents may have felt that their particular interests were not receiving sufficient (equal) weight in the decision-making process. This would be tantamount to suggesting that some in public office were acting unprofessionally, or, indeed, that their conduct was illegal. Second, and related to the issue raised above, any process of project evaluation undertaken without cost-benefit analysis is very much a political one where the criterion for acceptance (or otherwise) is not transparent. Such a process, therefore, is not easily questioned by those for whom it was initially established. The final hypothesis raised here is one of a process of change generated by the governmental agencies themselves. These agencies, charged with the task of conflict resolution, between taxpayers and benefit recipients, may have felt the need to be seen to be adopting open and innovative approaches to this issue. The motivation underpinning this final hypothesis could be said to be generated either from a positive, professional stance where new techniques are recognised and adopted because they are thought to enhance the service given to the public or, alternatively, from a negative point of view where the techniques are adopted for fear of criticism otherwise.

Whatever the rationale for change, and it may have been eclectic in its source of motivation, the overriding concepts inherent in the move towards the use of cost-benefit analysis were of transparency of decision making and a formal inclusion of all affected parties in the project evaluation process. Adoption of either, or both, of these concepts in decision making should be seen as a move toward facilitating greater public involvement. Such involvement in the context of the development of local plans, the relevant context here, is referred to as public participation.

The concept of participation has, however, over the life of cost-benefit analysis taken very different forms but could be accurately described to have swung between active and passive participation. Attempts at the former, active participation, were, and are, seen in such activities as public meetings. More recently, the use of direct valuation techniques, such as the contingent valuation method, might correctly be placed in this category. Sadly though, for the majority of its formalised history, cost-benefit analysis has been characterised by the contradictory concept of passive participation. Even in instances where active participation was easily within the grasp of analysts, the opportunity was not taken. An example of such is found in one of the earliest cost-benefit analysis studies in the UK, that of the siting of the proposed third London airport (Roskill (1970)). Those who would be asked to move due to the proposed development were not given (more) perfect information upon which to base their opinions. Instead, and as Mishan (1970) has argued, imperfect information in this instance led respondents to answer inaccurately the questions relating to the consumer's surplus of their homes. Underestimation of consumer's surplus was caused by respondents' believing they would only have to move locally in order to accommodate the hypothetical development with which they were presented. Of course, the noise nuisance which would have been generated by the operations at an airport was a localised problem which, in order to be avoided, would have necessitated a wider dispersion of the local community than was envisaged at the time by respondents. Participation was tried but it failed and it is interesting to consider why this may have been so.

First, it is possible that those undertaking the study, the 'experts' (and academics should be included in this category), would have had a much diminished responsibility in terms of interpreting responses if true, or active, participation had taken place. Second, it may be that the concept of 'expert opinion' is safe for decision makers. Thirdly, there appears to be an inherent reluctance by those charged with making decisions to accept that ordinary people might know best, or at least know better than the so-called experts. Instead of facilitators, analysts become dominant, their role being as 'gatekeepers' of vital information in the decision-making process.

It seems, then, that the pendulum of participation started, theoretically at least, on the active side. The general public should be included, their preferences should count, the outcome of project evaluation should be optimal for society and the process and criteria used in reaching a decision should be transparent and open to questioning and reinterpretation. Laudable objectives, but in practice, it would seem, difficult to implement. Given the vested interests in controlling the decision process discussed above, and especially in the early years of the development of the valuation techniques used in cost-benefit analysis, there was little motivation, and few tools available, to facilite active public participation.

Nowhere was this disenfranchizing more evident than in the range of valuation techniques developed by economists for estimating the intensity of feeling of those affected by a policy. Two principal techniques used for such valuation purposes have been the travel cost approach (Clawson (1959)) and the hedonic pricing method developed by, amongst others, Rosen (1974). Both of these techniques exemplify the indirect approach to valuation. Here, values are inferred by experts from actual, observed market-based information. Preferences, and, most importantly, the intensity of those preferences, are gauged by studying people's behavior patterns with regard to the good in question. In the travel cost approach, for instance, the distance travelled to, typically, a recreation facility is taken to represent how intensely that visitor values the facility. With a few provisos, the rule is basically that, the greater the distance travelled, the greater the inferred value for that facility. This is an interesting form of participation. Where the objective is to estimate the loss of welfare resulting from the closure of such a facility, visitors are not asked to gauge this themselves but rather experts do this on their behalf. Even though the experts, or their representatives, must conduct a survey on-site with the visitors, the latter are not given all the available information. Thus, visitors cannot inform the decision makers about their true value for the amenity (the full extent of any consumer's surplus) and thus the participation here must be seen as passive. A full discussion of this and other valuation techniques, along with a definition of total economic value, is provided in Chapter 3, but it is worth noting here that the passive participation referred to above is also restricted to the users of the facility. Non-users, but nonetheless people who may value the facility, are, by definition, excluded.

Theory would dictate that the pendulum of participation should swing toward the active end of the spectrum. In practice, however, the opposite, a passive approach to participation, seems to prevail. It is not even the case that these two opposing influences counter-balance one another, leaving the overall process in some satisfactory, but nonetheless suboptimal, equilibrium. Instead, the theory as espoused in the literature suggests that cost-benefit analysis does provide a voice for the public, and a voice with a volume control, whereas the techniques which are often used in valuation condemn the process to be categorized as passive participation. Until the relatively recent acceptance of a direct approach to valuation, the contingent valuation method, there has been a divergence between analysts talking about participation and analysts attempting to facilitate that participation. The advent of this new technique is important in terms of its pull on the 'practical' pendulum. There is now an opportunity for both the theory and the practice of participation to coincide, and for participation to be truly active.

A move towards active public participation, that is participation facilitated but not dominated by experts and bureaucratic procedures, is a central theme here. Cost-benefit analysis and, more particularly, valuation, may be used for various purposes including project (policy) appraisal, damage assessment for instance in compensation claims and, more straightforwardly, as a surrogate referendum mechanism. Given this latter use, cost-benefit analysis actually avoids the need for repeated referenda by adopting sample surveys. With a greater degree of active participation, valuations used in any of these contexts should produce better informed decisions. However, it is not just in the obtaining of a final valuation where active participation could prove useful. The process of participation is also important and, by using a direct valuation technique, the feeling of ownership of the process and final decision is to some extent transferred to those standing to gain or lose from a proposal.

Whilst global warming, ozone depletion and other environmental issues of major importance tend to capture the political agenda, the local environment is possibly the most noticeable area where the vast majority of the population experience incremental reductions in environmental quality. This local level is arguably the most appropriate one for the facilitation of active public participation. It is also at this level that, historically, planners rather than the public have determined developments and furthermore, it is an area which has hitherto managed to escape from the rigours of cost-benefit analysis. More than two decades ago, Dasgupta and Pearce (1972) observed that;

> The town planner, for example, is frequently without any systematic criteria, save his own paternalistic preferences. (p 15)

The situation is not very different now and this isolation of planners is evidenced by the work of Blowers *et al.* (1993). Their report to the Town and Country Planning Association on sustainable development in planning does not carry any reference to the concept of valuation nor to the work of economists such as Turner (1993) on sustainability. In another Report, DoE (1991) it is suggested that whilst the views of the public should be taken into account;

> .... in practice pressures of time and problems of confidentiality may restrict the amount of consultation ....

Some of the issues raised above are revisited in Chapter 3. There, the contingent valuation method is assessed against the requirements that a technique be able to elicit monetized individual preferences, that it minimises strategic behaviour in the elicitation procedure and that it engenders a feeling of ownership of decisions via 'active' participation in the process.

1.3 Overall Aims and Objectives

Overall, there are three aims to be addressed. The first is to establish the nature and extent of the problems that exist in the current practice of public participation in the context of the development of local plans. The second aim is to develop and test a means of improving these procedures. Finally, in order to gain acceptance of the proposed improvements, to consider the constraints of affordability and cost-effectiveness given that the relevant context is one of the development of local plans often involving financially constrained district, or city, councils.

The objectives in Chapter 2 are twofold. First, as suggestions for improvement of the participation process are based on an extension of the application of the contingent valuation method, a review is provided of the role of such survey-based techniques in the development of local plans. This is followed by an examination of current public participation policy and practice which fulfils the second of the two objectives for this chapter. Current policy is reviewed using the results of a questionnaire mailed to all 365 Chief Planning Officers in England and Wales. A principal focus of concern there is the extent to which an individual's intensity of feeling towards, or against, some policy is taken into account by planning officers. Where it is thought, by planners, that intensity of feeling is being taken fully into account, the basis for so doing is also examined. Thus, Chapter 2 addresses the first overall aim.

Given that the improvements to the public participation process suggested here are based on the adoption of the concept of valuation, and on the contingent valuation method in particular, Chapter 3 provides a comprehensive review of the development, theoretical underpinning and best practice of this technique. In relation to a definition of total economic value, the contingent valuation method is assessed alongside other valuation methods *viz* the travel cost approach and hedonic pricing method. The principal problems associated with the contingent valuation method are explored, detailing, for example, a number of reasons why willingness to pay for environmental improvements would be expected to differ from willingness to accept compensation for equivalent reductions in quality or quantity. Chapter 3 constitutes the substantive theoretical underpinning of the chosen method of preference elicitation.

Section 3.6 and Chapter 4 combine to meet the requirements of the third overall aim, that of developing a technique for public participation which is affordable for planning authorities and one which is cost-effective. This is achieved by using Lancaster's (1966) attribute theory which may then be applied to the valuation of a proposed local plan. Factorial survey design, introduced in Chapter 4, provides the basis of a vignette analysis approach which could be used to elicit values which are attached to the components of vignettes (or vectors) of attributes of a local plan. In essence, it is suggested that these vectors of attributes be reconstructed according to the unique, but similar, characteristics of other, geographically removed, local plans. Such an approach is likened to the developing practice of benefit transfer, a full discussion of which is provided in Section 3.6.

Chapter 5 provides a worked example of a transferable benefit estimate exercise. Building on the findings in Chapter 2, the theory detailed in Chapters 3 and 4 is combined to elicit and compare values from two samples drawn from the same population for proposals in an actual planning area, the Bristol North Fringe.

Finally, in Chapter 6, the most important issues arising from this work are reiterated, along with suggestions for improvement and further research.

2 Public Participation in Developing Local Plans

2.0 Introduction

According to Webster and Lavers (1991), relatively little research has been published on the issue of public participation in the planning process since the waning of the surge of interest in the 1970s following the Skeffington Report (1969). They suggest (p 813) that the paucity of publications in this field may be due to the fact that 'all is well' with public participation. Their review of the Barnet Unitary Development Plan, considered in Section 2.2, and other evidence discussed in Section 2.3 would suggest otherwise.

In the Skeffington Report (paragraph 80) it states:

> .... officers should be appointed to secure the involvement of those people who do not join organisations .... to work with people, to stimulate discussion, to inform people and give people's views to the authority.

This comment provides an example of the principal theme of the Report, recognising who planning is for and finding ways of encouraging participation in the planning process wherever relevant and possible.

In essence, the aim of this chapter is to illustrate some of the shortcomings of current public participation procedures. This is achieved by relating evidence of current practice to both the on-going debates in social choice theory discussed in Chapter 1 and to the more practical, process-oriented criticisms eminating from professional and academic planners.

In the next section consideration is given to the role of surveys in various planning models developed throughout this century. As the contingent valuation method forms the basis of recommended improvements to the public participation process, it is important to understand the likely degree of planners' familiarity with such preference elicitation surveys. Section 2.2 provides a summary of recent developments in, and contemporary criticisms of, public participation exercises. These criticisms relate, principally, to the procedural aspects of public participation rather than the theoretical imperatives discussed in Chapter 1. Such theoretical considerations are raised in the final section which provides additional comment on current practice as highlighted by the results of a questionnaire survey reported in Section 2.3.

2.1 The Evolution of Planning Models

This section provides a brief overview of the evolution of planning models from the early, simple, Geddesian 'Survey-before-Plan' procedure (Geddes 1915) to the current complex and dynamic 'Cyclical Strategic Choice Process', (Friend and Hickling 1987). The concepts developed in these two papers are the earliest and most recent of a range of models adopted by planners throughout the twentieth century which are described in some detail by Muller (1992).

Whilst Britain's Housing and Town Planning Act of 1909 laid the foundation stone for planning methods, it failed to offer a prescription in respect of the approach to be adopted in the preparation of plans. It was this omission which led Geddes to develop his simple model prescribing a survey stage before the plan is developed.

```
┌─────────┐
│ SURVEY  │
└────┬────┘
     │
   ┌─┴─┐
   │ B │
   │ E │
   │ F │
   │ O │
   │ R │
   │ E │
   └─┬─┘
     │
┌────┴────┐
│  PLAN   │
└─────────┘
```

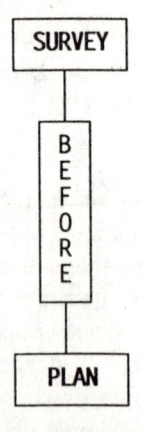

Figure 2.1 The Geddesian Model

It is this relatively simple concept that the majority of users of market research employ today. Businesses survive by adapting to the changing needs of their customers by using a variety of feedback mechanisms and, likewise, planners must adapt to the changing needs of citizens. As Healey (1990) states:

> The major democratic movement of the late twentieth century .... challenges the capacity and desirability of politicians, bureaucrats and technocrats to act 'for' citizens guided by some superior knowledge of what 'people' want and 'the public interest'. People no longer trust experts to define their interests for them. (p 21)

The 'survey' as a feedback mechanism has been an integral part of all the major planning methods which have followed from the Geddesian model. Muller (1992) states that Geddes' survey system was comprehensive ranging from population data, communications and manufacturing data to geology and even climatology for wider or longer plans. However no mention is made of surveys of citizens' preferences. It is the absence of data on this seemingly fundamental input to the planning process which led to the dismissal of the Geddesian model. Authors such as Birch (1980) and McLoughlin (1969) have provided critical comment on the lack of objectives for the data collection stage advocated by Geddes.

According to Breheny and Batey (1981) the lack of objectives for the survey stage in the Geddesian model resulted in other models prescribing pre-survey surveys and others seeking clarification on the objectives themselves through an open formulation process. However, even with such incremental developments towards a more informed and participative planning process, during the first half of the century there was still no explicit reference to the inclusion of the general public's preferences.

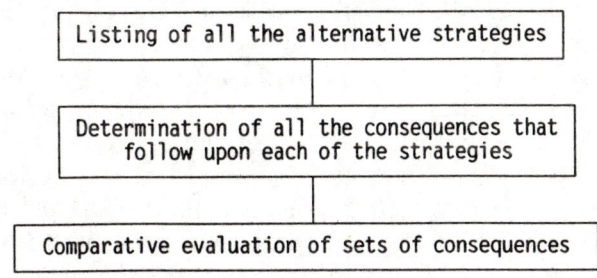

```
┌─────────────────────────────────────────────┐
│  Listing of all the alternative strategies  │
└─────────────────────────────────────────────┘
                      │
┌─────────────────────────────────────────────┐
│  Determination of all the consequences that │
│       follow upon each of the strategies    │
└─────────────────────────────────────────────┘
                      │
┌─────────────────────────────────────────────┐
│  Comparative evaluation of sets of consequences │
└─────────────────────────────────────────────┘
```

Figure 2.2 Simon's Decision Model
Source: Simons (1965)

In the early 1960s Simon (1965) began to introduce the concept of rationality into the planning literature. In conjunction with March he also introduced the supplementary theme of bounded rationality (March and Simon (1959)). Simon's decision model (Figure 2.2) is the first planning model to incorporate the principles of neo-classical economics. In effect, the process implied by the model suggests a form of **cost-benefit analysis** although no mention is given of the ways and means to 'comparative evaluation' in the final stage.

Around the same time, Davidoff and Reiner (1962) were developing their ideas of efficiency and rationality in the planning process culminating in their model of Choice Theory presented in Figure 2.3.

```
┌─────────────────────────────────────────┐
│ Value formulation:                      │
│ Responsibility, analysis and evaluation │
└─────────────────────────────────────────┘
                  │
┌─────────────────────────────────────────┐
│ Means identification:                   │
│ Alternative choice and weighting        │
└─────────────────────────────────────────┘
                  │
┌─────────────────────────────────────────┐
│ Effectuation:                           │
│ Directed and automatic controls         │
└─────────────────────────────────────────┘
```

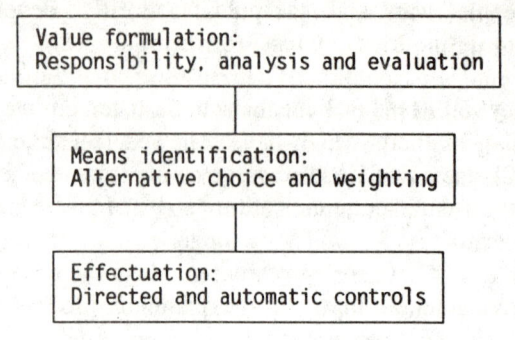

Figure 2.3 Choice Theory
Source: Davidoff and Reiner (1962)

Here again, the principles of neo-classical economics appear in the process. According to Muller (1992), Davidoff and Reiner sought to measure efficiency defined as the satisfaction of aggregated individual preferences. In the second stage of their model, that of 'means identification' the authors also refer to weighting various alternatives, but do not specify an adequate means of so doing.

From this point onwards, there is an increased degree of complexity in the planning models developed in the literature. Two major developments were made. Firstly, in the Systems Approach, as described by McLoughlin (1969), planners started to incorporate past experience, evaluation of previous decisions before embarking on the linear sequential process of developing the next plan. The contribution from Strategic Choice theorists such as Friend and Hickling (1987) has been to illustrate that planning is not a linear sequential process but instead a continuous and multi-faceted process with constant input and feedback to and from various actors within it. However, the inclusion of an 'evaluation of alternative strategies' stage and a 'weighting of various outcomes' stage are common. The former is usually an explicit stage whereas the latter, whilst often left unmentioned, also forms an integral part of the decision process, if only by default. For instance, if no account is taken of distributional issues arising from various alternative strategies then an implicit unitary weighting is being used for all affected parties.

In all the models discussed above, the survey stages have focused primarily on demographic and socio-economic aspects. It was not until the 1960s onwards that significant recognition was given to the need to directly seek the general public's participation in the process.

Many authors such as Godschalk and Mills (1966), Burke (1968), Arnstein (1969), Sewell and Coppock (1977), Alty and Darke (1987), Blackman (1991a, 1991b) and Healey and Gilroy (1991) have developed the ideas of public participation. These developments are discussed in Section 2.2.

This section has sought to demonstrate that surveys have been a recommended tool of the planner for at least as long as the Geddesian model has been employed. Whilst models have become increasing complex and comprehensive it is only relatively recently that the preferences of the general public have been explicitly sought.

2.2 Recent Developments in Public Participation

There have been two complementary themes running through the public participation literature since the early 1970s. These are, first, a concern with the role, timing and scope of public participation within the planning procedure. The second is a focus on the research methods employed in public participation.

In a wider sense, the general planning literature also contains a political dimension (for example, see Thornley (1977)) which examines, amongst other things, the procedures for, and methods of, public participation as political tools for achieving social aims, be they change or stability.

This case is argued strongly in the literature but it is not dealt with directly here. Instead, the focus of this section is an examination of the procedures for, and methods of, public participation. Evidence of a lack of public participation, or of procedures inhibiting such participation, would of course lend support to, but not constitute proof of, Thornley's case. However, when the issue of 'weighting' of responses in public participation exercises is considered, the political dimension raised by Thornley may be relevant. It would seem that social aims can be, and have been, used to determine the deservedness of (and thus weightings for) various socio-economic groups affected by public policy decisions. Currently, no explicit weighting mechanism is used and Webster and Lavers (1991) even found evidence of weightings being determined after the Public Local Inquiry Stage. Written objections, it was decided, would be assigned a lower weighting than verbal representations. Section 2.4 provides some comments on current practice on this topic.

Arnstein's (1969) typology of participation (Figure 2.4), as a ladder consisting of eight rungs ranging from 'manipulation' to 'citizen control' is useful as a framework for examining the current status of participation. It is not enough to show that opportunities for participation exist in order to say that participation actually takes place. The opportunity is necessary but not sufficient. According to Alty and Darke (1987) and Healey and Gilroy (1990) the early 1970s were characterised by blind-alley opportunities. Where a local authority instigated a public participation programme it was, according to Alty and Darke,

> .... seen as a good thing of itself. The outcome was often an uncoordinated and incoherent set of interventions and programme elements which provided ambiguous or inadequate information. (p7)

They go on to cite examples of costly exercises undertaken to gather relevant information but where the resources were not available for abstracting, summarising and disseminating the results. Even by 1986, Alty and Darke show that the Sheffield Central Area planning exercise resulted in little more than consultation (rung 4, Figure 2.4) which Arnstein herself described as a 'sham' and 'window dressing'.

The opportunity for public participation invariably stems from a statutory requirement from central government. However, whilst the Skeffington Report (1969) stated that:

> .... we have been urged to recommend that the public should be involved from the start in the establishment of the broad aims or goals that the community wish to see achieved ....

in the same report it is concluded simply that:

> we doubt the necessity for that in this country. (p 24, para 136).

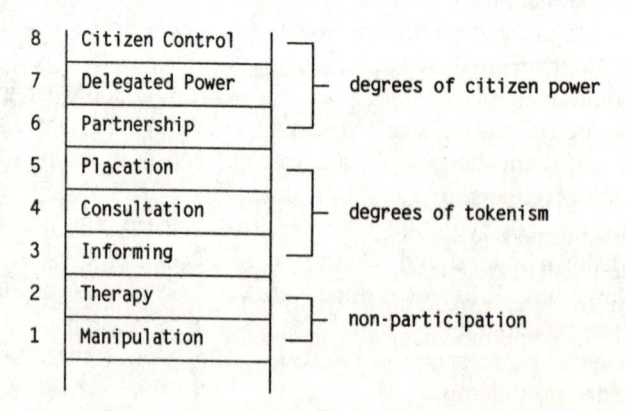

8	Citizen Control	
7	Delegated Power	degrees of citizen power
6	Partnership	
5	Placation	
4	Consultation	degrees of tokenism
3	Informing	
2	Therapy	non-participation
1	Manipulation	

Figure 2.4 Eight Rungs on a Ladder of Citizen Participation
Source: Arnstein (1969)

Even though in 1973 the Department of the Environment supported experimental surveys of the public's views during the wider, Structure Plan stage of the planning process (Hedges (1976)), currently, such public participation need not necessarily take place. It is only in the development of local plans that local planning authorities have a statutory requirement for public participation.[1] This runs contrary to the views of Kweit and Kweit (1987) who suggest that participation should take place at the stage where the community decides where it wants to go, not how it should get there. Choosing the means is important, but defining the ends is even more so. Furthermore, if the use of monetized preferences is advocated, Norgaard (1986) concludes that economic valuation techniques are best suited to broad strategy evaluation rather than to fine tuning.

Bruton and Nicholson (1987) summarise the relevant responsibility of the local planning authority as:

1) to give adequate publicity in the area to the matters proposed to be included in the plan,
2) to give those interested an adequate opportunity to make representations and
3) to make them (the public) aware of these opportunities. (p158)

Until February 1992, when the Government (DoE (1992)) published new guidelines on the appropriate length of the consultation period, local authorities were expected to undertake at least six weeks for this exercise. The 1992 guidelines are less precise leaving the extent and length of the exercise to the judgment of local authorities. Bruton and Nicholson go on to recognise that whilst the DoE advised that authorities could undertake further work than the minimum requirement entails, it must only be undertaken where the authority is satisfied that the additional work and delay involved is clearly justified.

Two recent studies have sought to gauge the pre 1992 statutory requirements in terms of Arnstein's ladder as shown in Figure 2.4. Webster and Lavers (1991) state that the Local Public Inquiry is the principal formal mechanism for public participation in both unitary development plans and district-wide local plans. Their review of the Barnet Unitary Development Plan, from an objector's point of view, places this process firmly in Arnstein's category of tokenism. As already mentioned, Alty and Darke's (1987) review of the Sheffield Central Area Plan gave a similar result. The impact of the 1992 guidelines has been to reduce the resources applied to

---

[1] Structure Plans provide overall guidance for the development of a community. Local Plans provide the detail of how the Structure Plan is to be implemented.

public participation. It is likely then that these recent changes have forced public participation even further down the 'ladder of citizen participation'.

Whilst these comments present a bleak picture of the role of public participation in the planning process, Blackman (1991a, 1991b) and Healey and Gilroy (1990), have suggested that the true picture is even less encouraging. In his Study of Belfast, Blackman (1991b) found that the concept of referendum, (the term used by the Planning Appeals Commission to refer to consideration of the views of local people), was dismissed;

> .... since the motivation of objectors is an important consideration and the crucial test of the acceptability of a planning application is whether or not the proposed development would do harm to interests of acknowledged importance. (p 35)

Blackman concludes that, in the Belfast case, the values of people directly affected by a proposed development were considered to be suspect. Those of the speculative developer however, even though he was cited as acquiring the site because it 'suited his pocket', were regarded as valid.

Healey and Gilroy's (1990) criticism of public participation focuses on the communication between planner and public. They argue that the language used and the style of documentation produced by planners does not lend itself to be used by the general public.

Webster and Lavers (1991) provide further evidence of the difficulties individuals face in the participatory procedures. Quite simply, they conclude that few individuals can represent themselves at Public Local Inquiries purely because these meetings are usually held during normal working hours.

These further arguments lend support to the hypothesis that the role of public participation in planning is far from ideal. Two possible solutions exist. Firstly a review of the current system of representative democracy where community or pressure groups take on a more professional and accountable role. Such a move was tried in Belfast where an organisation, Community Technical Aid (CTA), was established to assist community groups in the planning process. The state's lack of commitment to this scheme however can be seen in the £50,000 grant made available to CTA compared with £1.2 million spent on consultant's reports for the plan (Blackman (1991b) p 13).

The second solution relies on the success of extending the role of direct democracy. Whereas direct democracy has in the past been seen as unwieldy, costly and ineffective, progress in survey techniques and data processing have provided new opportunities for direct participation.

Progress of this second solution also breathes new life into cost-benefit approaches to planning (Schofield (1987)) and the use of the planning balance sheet (PBS), (Lichfield (1964)). The former evaluates a plan by assigning monetary values to all the changes on all affected parties resulting from some project. The PBS approach follows the identical procedure for those changes which are easily quantifiable in money terms. For other affects, a qualitative description is proposed. With the development of more rigorous valuation techniques the PBS approach merely moves closer to the cost-benefit approach as the qualitative becomes quantifiable.

It is not being argued here that monetary valuations should replace the public participation process as it currently operates. Instead, and as Alty and Darke (1987) recommend, any programme of public participation must include a range of techniques and approaches if it is to be more than tokenist.

Given the array of target groups which would be included in a comprehensive public participation programme and the evidence of exclusion of certain groups in the Sheffield, Barnet and Belfast Studies reviewed in this section (Alty and Darke (1987), Webster and Lavers (1991), Blackman (1991a, 1991b)), it is suggested that there is a role for a proactive survey approach to be used by planners. Even though participatory critics note the increased costs, time and potential for conflict, Kweit and Kweit (1987) assert that the process will lead to enhanced decision-making. This trade-off between additional resources at the input and analysis stages and more efficient decision making as an output should be considered especially in light of the current, seemingly unsatisfactory process of public participation that has been described in this section.

2.3 Public Participation - Some Current Practices

In this section, the results of a questionnaire survey mailed to all Chief Planning Officers in England and Wales are reported. The questionnaires were mailed in July 1992. A total of 365 recipients were identified. At the time of analysis, August 1992, 246 responses had been received representing a response rate of 67%. Questions posed are reported in the text and the complete questionnaire is shown as Appendix 1. The analysis was conducted using the SPSS-PC software.

Due to the fact that not all local authorities had been through the whole plan development process, and also that not all questions were completed by all respondents, the percentages reported here are calculated using valid responses only. (The number (n), of valid responses is shown alongside each case.)

In the piloting stage of the questionnaire design, four stages were identified where the general public are given the opportunity to participate in the development of a local plan. These are the:

1) Informal Consultation Draft (ICD),
2) Deposit Consultation (DC),
3) Inquiry or Examination in Public (IEP) and
4) Consultation on Modifications (CM).

It was an objective of the survey to examine current practice at each of these stages. Current practice covers:

i) informing the general public,
ii) presenting the plan to the general public,
iii) receiving responses from the general public,
vi) weighting given to responses from different members of the general public,
v) overall importance of general public responses as perceived by planners, and
vi) changes to a local plan due to the public participation exercise.

Table 2.1
Informing the General Public

Q1 How are the *general public* informed of the participation/consultation exercise at each of the stages listed?

(please tick as appropriate : you may tick more than one box per stage)

STAGE	E	PM	N	T	R	
Informal Consultation Draft	87	69	97	12	48	n = 242
Deposit Consultation	48	28	97	9	37	n = 209
Inquiry or Examination in Public	9	7	91	7	23	n = 187
Consultations on Modifications	32	9	90	5	14	n = 166

Percentage of respondents using each method

E (Exhibitions), PM (Public Meetings), N (Newspapers), T (Television), R (Radio)

A number of inferences can be drawn from the data in Table 2.1. Firstly, it would seem that the range of media used to inform the public of the development of a local plan reduces as the stages of development progress. There may be good reason for this. Wide coverage at the initial stage may be sufficient to generate interest which can then be sustained using fewer, more cost-effective, lines of communication. It was also noted by many respondents that it is quite valid for fewer lines of communication with the public to be used in the later stages. At these later stages, individual letters are sent to those who objected at the Draft Stage. However, it would seem that if the public do not register as objectors at the Draft Stage, they have little chance of participating in later stages.

Not one respondent indicated that a proactive stance to direct public participation was adopted. On no occasion was it stated that officers sought public opinion by going out to the public. The public is expected to come to them. Opportunity to participate was created but that opportunity does not guarantee a representative cross-section of views.

One respondent commented,

> The public are not involved - except as objectors - and it's impossible to contact the general public - unless they come forward.

This would seem to show an ignorance, or dismissal, of market research type survey techniques. Secondly, it should be noted that at each stage, over 90 percent of respondents used newspapers to carry their message. Where television and radio were used, respondents generally indicated that press releases about the plan were issued. There was no guarantee of coverage. No respondents indicated explicitly that air time was bought. Fewer than half, 42 percent, sent a direct communication to every household.

Other frequently used methods include posters, public notices and both leaflet drops and leaflet points in public areas.

Given both the financial and social consequences arising from the implementation of a local plan, surprisingly little use is made of either direct communications to households or of the more penetrating television media. Whilst the latter is relatively expensive, effectiveness, and probably therefore expenditure, ought to be commensurate with the likely consequences of a plan.

From inspection of Table 2.2, there appears to be a wider cross-section of techniques used in the earlier rather than later stages. Other principal themes are the reliance on newspapers throughout to meet statutory requirements and the rapidly decreasing use of both exhibitions and public meetings as the plan is progressed.

Table 2.2
Presenting Plans to the General Public

Q3 Which form of media is used to present the plan to the *general public* at each stage?

(please tick as appropriate : you may tick more than one box per stage)

STAGE	\multicolumn{8}{c}{Percentage of respondents using each method}
	M	Eo	E	PM	N	T	V	R	
Informal Consultation Draft	53	88	42	62	78	5	14	27	n = 241
Deposit Consultation	34	38	33	23	72	3	2	21	n = 208
Inquiry or Examination in Public	17	9	9	7	67	4	2	10	n = 186
Consultations on Modifications	19	14	16	9	70	4	2	11	n = 165

M   -   Mail including leaflet drop or council newsletter with invitation to reply
PM -   Public Meeting minuted
R   -   Radio with invitation to reply
Eo   -   Exhibition with Officers, forms available for reply
N   -   Newspaper with invitation to reply
V   -   Video with invitation to reply
E   -   Exhibition without officers, forms available for reply
T   -   Television with invitation to reply

Table 2.3 reveals that, predominantly, responses are received predominantly in writing, with more respondents indicating that these are received on official forms rather than in non-official format. Telephone and face-to-face contact are used significantly less than a written format. Interestingly, examination of official response sheets indicates that they offer little in the way of allowing expression of intensity of feeling on behalf of the respondent. Such intensity of feeling needs to be inferred by officers charged with analysing these response sheets. This issue is explored further under the heading of 'weighting' below.

Around 50 percent of the sample of planners stated that, in their view, there was not an acceptable level of response from a wide enough cross-section of the general public. This was true at each stage and is more strongly supported at the later stages.

Table 2.3
Receiving Responses from the General Public

Q4 At each stage, how are the majority of responses from the *general public* received?

(please tick as appropriate : you may tick more than one box per stage if responses are equally split between 2 or more categories)

Percentage of respondents receiving majority of responses via:					
STAGE	ML	MF	P	C	
Informal Consultation Draft	70	74	9	17	n = 242
Deposit Consultation	39	83	5	6	n = 209
Inquiry or Examination in Public	37	61	2	6	n = 187
Consultations on Modifications	41	62	5	4	n = 166

ML - Mail (non-official form), MF - Mail (official form), P - Telephone,
C - Notes from face-to-face conversation with officer

Table 2.4
Gauging Intensity of Feeling

Q6 How is the *general public's* intensity of feeling towards any aspect of the plan calculated at each stage?

(please tick one box per stage)

	Percentage of respondents who 'weight' by each method:				
STAGE	1. no. of responses	2. tone of responses	3. status of respondents	4. Quality of response	5. Some Combination of 1,2,3,4
Informal Consultation Draft	17	3	0	5	75
Deposit Consultation	13	3	0	8	75
Inquiry or Examination in Public	12	4	0	15	69
Consultations on Modifications	13	5	0	13	69

Table 2.4 illustrates that between 12 and 17 percent of planners who responded (depending on the stage), gauge the intensity of public feeling solely by the number of responses received on specific issues. As a plan progresses, an increasing number rely on the quality of response. As might be expected, the vast majority use a combination of methods. Whilst respondents were not asked to expand their answers if they ticked the 'combination' column, many did. It appears that very few of those using a combination of methods relied to any extent on the status of the respondent. Instead, there is a tendency towards the number and quality of responses.

Relying on the number of responses is analogous to a voting system. As such, it fails to provide an adequate representation of intensity of feeling. Furthermore, reliance on the quality of response is very much a subjective judgement with officers having to infer intensity of feeling normally by how well researched or articulated a response may be.

Some comments from respondents with regard to the weighting issue are reported below:

Intensity of feeling - this is a difficult issue - you can only really judge feelings from the actual responses you receive. There is a danger of 'reading-in' too much extra.
Depends on depth of argument and quality of evidence.
.... officers look at the arguments themselves (intensity of feeling is not significant).
.... judged by the number of people willing to attend public meetings.
Intensity of feeling is not a material planning consideration.

As discussed in Section 1.1, one of the reasons why Arrow (1953) turned towards ordinal expressions of preference was because of the discretionary power in the hands of public servants wherever cardinal measures were used. According to Mueller (1989), Arrow's concern of potential malpractice could be avoided by eliciting weightings directly from respondents. A monetary-based, cardinal measure of intensity of preference is one means of achieving this end.

Forty one percent of respondents thought that certain community or commercial groups were given a more than average opportunity to participate in the development of a plan. These were generally stated to be: Parish Councils, housebuilders, amenity societies and representatives of trade and industry.

The trend evident in Table 2.5 is one of a decreasing importance attached to the preferences of the general public as a plan is progressed. By the final stage, over one quarter of respondents stated that 'Little', 'Very Little' or 'No' importance was attached.

Table 2.5
The Degree of Importance Attached to Preferences of the General Public

Q9 In your view, how much importance is given to the preferences of the *general public* at each stage?

(please tick one box per stage)

STAGE	Percentage of respondents indicating level of importance:					
	Significant	Some	Little	Very Little	None	
Informal Consultation Draft	60	34	3	1	3	n = 234
Deposit Consultation	44	50	3	2	2	n = 190
Inquiry or Examination in Public	43	37	11	4	5	n = 159
Consultations on Modifications	34	38	14	10	4	n = 146

Around 10 percent of respondents at each stage indicated that the level of importance attached to the preferences of the general public was inadequate. The principal constraints to improving the process were seen to be 'Public Apathy' and 'Financial'.

A local plan as presented to the general public may be highly acceptable to them. In this case, it would be expected that public participation would lead to few changes in the plan. However, respondents were also asked to indicate the level of revision to a plan due to the public participation exercise. Out of the 194 valid responses, 15 percent stated that the process did not lead to any changes in the plan. 26 percent indicated solely 'Few minor' changes. A further 16 percent experienced 'Many minor' revisions. One third of respondents found that public participation led to Minor revisions but were unable to distinguish between 'many' and a 'few'. In all then, 90 percent saw the effects of public participation resulting in minor or no changes to a local plan. Only 1 percent indicated 'Many major' revisions.

2.4 A Rationale for the Use of Contingent Valuation in the Participatory Process

The previous sections have sought to illustrate the degree to which the views of the general public are taken into account in the planning process. The mechanisms and timing of these procedures were also critically appraised. In this section, the principal weaknesses of current practice are reiterated and considered in the light of Arrow's (1953) work. The outcome provides a rationale for looking towards new techniques and procedures in a bid to alleviate these problems.

In 1977, O'Riordan stated that:

> Probably the single most pressing difficulty facing participation is the involvement of the citizenry at large. At present most of the standard techniques such as hearings, task forces, etc., do not appear to be suitable for people concerned with local issues and day-to-day living. (p 169)

More recent conclusions drawn from case studies and discussed in Section 2.2 would suggest that this situation has not improved. Although from the responses to the questionnaire it was found that planning officers were, on the whole, satisfied with current practice, the comments drawn from the case studies suggest that objectors and the general public are far from content. The review of current practice reported in that section, especially on issues such as weighting, also tends to highlight areas for concern.

In Chapter 1, Arrow's impossibility theorem was discussed along with a rationale for reverting to cardinal measures of individuals' preferences. It was argued there that even though the use of cardinal scales may constitute imperfect practice, the alternatives are also open to criticism. One of Arrow's major concerns with the implementation of the concept of cardinality was that the interpretation of intensity of feeling may be determined by public servants. Indeed, the review of this issue in the previous section suggests that this is the norm in the planning process. Where some planners deviate from this norm, the adopted practice appears to be one similar to a voting mechanism whereby objections to a plan are simply counted. Both of these approaches to the issue of weighting are flawed. The first requires a degree of subjectivity which will vary amongst planning officers and amongst planning authorities. The second, seemingly more objective, approach has a number of associated problems. The public, for instance, are not informed that such a vote-counting process will determine outcomes and they may, therefore, not bother to cast their vote. Where the public do suspect that such a process will operate there is potential for respondents to vote strategically. Also, it is only by coincidence that each objection should carry equal weight. In order to avoid, or at least reduce, the potential problems alluded to above, it is necessary to minimize the possibility of strategic behaviour and to use a technique, such as the contingent valuation method, to elicit intensity of preference directly from a respondent.

Given that many people failed to make use of the opportunities available to them for participation, and further that many of those who did participate found the procedures 'unfriendly', consideration should be given to different 'enabling' structures for the public participation process. Furthermore, as was seen in Section 2.3, 'public apathy' was held to be a constraint to improvements of the public participation process. Survey techniques, such as the contingent valuation method, tend to require less effort on behalf of the respondent as the process is taken to them.

Section 2.1 reviewed the role of surveys in planning. From the early Geddesian model onwards, surveys have played a part in planning as a means of generating inputs to the decision process. Surveys and data handling concepts are not new to planners and the addition of a monetized public preference elicitation technique such as the contingent valuation method must be seen as an incremental, rather than a radical, change in practice.

The development of planning models, including Davidoff and Reiner's (1962) choice theory and the more recent strategic choice models, also point towards the need for different survey techniques to be employed by planners. For example, in the former, choice theorists introduce the concept of rational decision making by assuming perfect information. From the studies reviewed in Section 2.2 this was not found to be the case with information presented to community representatives being too complex, and especially too technical, for lay people to comprehend its implications. Use of the contingent valuation method however, succeeds in enhancing the provision of information to respondents via detailed descriptions using photographs and even video.

Strategic choice theorists consider the planning process to be on-going, with many different influences affecting many different actors. However, rather, than continuously conducting site specific or plan specific valuations, which would encourage criticisms based on excessive cost and time delays, it may be more efficient to construct a 'bank' of valuations determined by respondent characteristics and site or plan characteristics. This is termed the 'piecewise independent valuation procedure' by Randall (1991) and is, essentially, the practice of benefit transfer discussed in Section 3.6. Such a valuation bank could be used with both cost-benefit analysis and planning balance sheet approaches to enhance public participation.

Whilst Kweit and Kweit (1987) advocate the use of cost-benefit analysis in planning procedures, they are sceptical about the likely commitment from planners to the increased public participation that this would entail. There are, they suggest, two principal disincentives for officials. Firstly, there would be an increase in costs and time demanded. Secondly, the use of cost-benefit analysis inevitably highlights the conflict between various groups in a community. Recognition of such conflict and the explicit trade-offs which must be made between such groups may, they suggest, lead to a reduction in the acceptance of policy. However, if a local environment does not develop satisfactorily due to a lack of public participation, the repercussions would be felt eventually.

3 Cost-effective Preference Revelation

3.0 Introduction

The discussion in Chapter 1 with regard to the debate which has ensued since Arrow (1951) published his impossibility theorem culminated in a number of requirements for a voting technique which would enhance public participation in public decision making. First, the technique would have to be capable of capturing intensity of preferences directly from members of the public. Preferences would thus need to be measured on a cardinal scale and in order to estimate the overall size of public spending on a particular issue, the scale should be money-based. As the concept of ownership of decision making was also seen as important, the technique should also include the public in what was termed an 'active' rather than a 'passive' manner. Other criteria demand that the technique be capable of minimizing strategic behaviour by respondents and that the results should lend themselves to sensitivity analysis. Taken as a whole, these criteria already form a stringent package. However, in the next section, where the concept of total economic value is explored, a further criterion is added. In order to estimate total economic value, both users and nonusers who value an amenity would need to be considered.

Advocates of the three main valuation techniques used in cost-benefit analysis, the travel cost approach, hedonic pricing and the contingent valuation method (CVM), would all claim to capture intensity of preference although, as was discussed in Chapter 1, only the latter can do so in a direct way. Further fundamental differences between these techniques in relation to the stated requirements lie in the varying ability of each to incorporate nonusers in the analysis and the varying degree of active involvement of respondents.

In deciding on the most appropriate technique there is also an issue of context to be considered. Given that an aim of this work is the improvement of public participation in the development of local plans, there is an obvious practical reason for preferring the direct method, the CVM, rather than either of the two indirect approaches. The travel cost approach would be inappropriate as the environmental amenity in question (green space) is within easy walking distance for the majority of the relevant population. The hedonic pricing method could prove more relevant than the travel cost approach but a good supply of house price data may not always be readily available. Other problems with the travel cost approach and hedonic pricing are discussed briefly in Section 3.2 before, in the subsequent sections, the CVM, as the preferred valuation technique, is explored in detail. The discussion of the CVM begins with a review of some aspects of welfare economics, namely the distinction between Marshallian and Hicksian consumer's surplus measures. Both indirect techniques estimate consumer's surplus using the Marshallian approach whereas the true measure of consumer's surplus, the income-adjusted Hicksian measure, is the outcome of using the CVM. Whilst some of the problems of using the indirect approaches have already been alluded to, it is also true that the CVM has some pitfalls and shortcomings. In Section 3.5 these problems, and the ways in which practitioners have dealt with them, are reviewed under the subsection headings of bias, validity and reliability. Section 3.6 provides a departure from this purely CVM focus as researchers in this field appear to have overlooked the links between tests of reliability and tests of the relatively new practice of benefit transfer. Benefit transfer provides the basis of the cost-effectiveness of the recommendations eminating from this work and, as such, that section provides a detailed look at both why benefit transfer has grown in popularity and how it has been, and is, conducted. This chapter ends with a summarized guide to good practice in the use of CVM alongwith some concluding thoughts on the appropriateness of using the CVM and benefit transfer as a means of enhancing public participation.

3.1 Total Economic Value - Categories of Benefits

Just who is likely to be affected by a proposed change in a local environment is a difficult issue to address. Most obviously, those who are to suffer from a new road or housing development next to where they live ought to be considered. Costs of compulsory purchase, for instance, do find their way into cost-benefit analyses but as the effects of development become less apparent, or more difficult to estimate, the temptation for analysts is to ignore them or to provide a qualitative assessment. Bateman *et al.* (1993) provide a good example of this scenario in their review of the UK government's cost-benefit analysis of road schemes. They conclude that no account is taken of environmental effects other than to list the consequences for consideration alongside monetized costs and benefits such as time savings.

However, just because it is difficult to identify those affected, and the degree to which they are affected, should not mean that such people are excluded from any analysis. A useful framework that has been developed by economists in order to identify all those likely to be affected by a proposal is that of total economic value. This simple framework which states that the total economic value is the sum of values held by both users and nonusers of an amenity provides an excellent basis for deciding on the sampling frame for a cost-benefit study, or indeed for those who ought to be consulted in a public participation exercise. The user and nonuser categories are explored in more detail later in this section but whilst it may seem obvious that all users of some amenity would be affected by a change to it, it was not until 1967 that Krutilla argued for the inclusion of non-priced leisure activities in the estimation of benefits derived from various waterways. Prior to that date, accounting practice was to include solely commercial freight and priced leisure activities.

Use values refer to benefits derived from both direct and indirect contact with the amenity in question. For example, Mitchell and Carson (1989) refer to a possible scenario where consideration is being given to an improvement in water quality at a particular location. Direct use values may be derived from 'in-stream' activities such as boating or from 'withdrawal', say an increase in drinking water quality. Indirect use values, they suggest, would accrue to those engaging in 'near-water' recreation and from 'ecosystem' developments supporting say, bird watching.

As an example of the relative size of non-priced recreational activities Willis and Garrod (1991) in a study of certain canals and waterways in the UK, estimated that non-commercial use values (both direct and indirect) outweighed the government grant of maintaining these amenities. Previous estimates of benefits relying on commercial activity alone had seriously undervalued such amenities.

Interestingly, in the conclusion to their paper, Willis and Garrod acknowledge the heterogeneous nature of individual sections of waterways and the varying levels of subsidies devoted to, and benefits derived from, these different sections. Varying levels of benefits derived from amenities with different attributes is not unexpected although this assertion is at variance with the results of Hanley and Ruffell's (1993) study of forest characteristics as the determinants of the level of welfare. Indeed, the practical advances that are being made in the process of benefit transfer (see Section 3.6) are becoming increasingly reliant on estimating the contribution of individual site characteristics to total economic value. Success in this area of research would allow for practical management decisions, with regard to subsidy levels, to be taken without the need for original 'site specific' studies to be undertaken in all cases.

While use benefits have been expanded in definition and valuation techniques have become increasingly sophisticated in order to measure this category, nonuse benefits as identified by Krutilla and Fisher (1975) have proved to be the source of much debate. Such debate has led Green and Tunstall (1991) to state that:

> In the absence to date of adequately empirically grounded theories of nonuse values, it is not possible to separate willingness to pay for use value from nonuse value without running serious risks of both double-counting and underestimation. (p1142)

However, what seems clear from the literature is a general acceptance of the existence of the nonuse class of benefits. Debate is now focused on what should constitute inclusion in this category of benefits and how each should be measured.

Randall (1991) suggests that nonuse values encompass the four separate categories of:

- Option value,
- Quasi-option value,
- Existence value and
- Vicarious use value.

Mitchell and Carson (1989), however, argue against the inclusion of option values on the grounds that such values are the result of uncertainty in either future use (demand side) or in future provision (supply side) of the environmental amenities in question. This uncertainty, they appear to argue, can be minimised with useful information provided to respondents and that option value should not be considered as a seperate benefit category but rather as a correction factor to calculations of total benefits. However, work by Sun *et al.* (1992) would tend to support the concept of option value. They provide a conceptual model for estimating option value for groundwater quality protection looking at the effects on the option value of varying the subjective demand and supply uncertainty. However, it is not clear from their work that they adequately separate option value from a respondent's perceived use value. By varying the subjective demand and supply uncertainty, Sun *et al.* were providing respondents with different types of information. Similar work was carried out by Fisher and Hanemann (1990) who have linked the concept of option value to that of the value of information.

Linked to the concept of option value is that of quasi-option value. In the latter, values are said to exist due to some people having a preference to preserve a habitat on the understanding that as time passes, information and knowledge about the possible uses of the habitat will increase. This argument is especially relevant when consideration is given to a total, rather than a marginal, change in an amenity. The extinction of a species for example means that possible future benefits derived from this source could never be enjoyed. Again, Mitchell and Carson are reluctant to accept this as a separate category of benefits and suggest that quasi-option value, like option value, need only be a correction factor in estimating total benefits.

However, correction factors still need to be estimated if total benefit estimation is to be accurate. The debate appears to be one of semantics or, more correctly, disagreement about how respondents should and do include option values in their willingness to pay bids. This is an aspect of the problem to which Green and Tunstall (1991) suggest care should be taken to avoid double-counting or underestimation.

The measurement of existence values appears to be equally contentious. Krutilla and Fisher (1975) argue that an individual's utility can be derived from an amenity without that person physically having to visit the amenity. This utility can be gained in two ways, from either anthropocentric or ecocentric standpoints. Firstly, utility could be derived from overlapping or interdependent utility functions either intragenerational or intergenerational. Here, one person's utility is dependent on that of others, either alive or yet to be born. Also plausible is the case of overlapping utility functions between those still alive and those who have died. Comments such as 'we owe it to our forbearers to protect...' suggest that significant historic sites especially, may provide an aspect of existence value dependent on previous rather than future generations. Other anthropocentric actions would include such things as the giving of a gift, leaving an amenity for the next generation, or helping to preserve an area for the benefit of the indigenous population.

The ecocentric arguments resulting in positive existence values are based on the utility derived from satisfaction of ethical standards including upholding the rights of non-humans. However, Brookshire *et al.* (1986) have argued that these ethically-based motivations should not be included in existence values because, they say, utility is not increased by such behaviour. Mitchell and Carson (1989) provide a useful critique of the work of Brookshire *et al.* stating that ethical motivations also underpin the anthropocentric actions mentioned previously. The work of animal rights activists would also suggest that the conclusions drawn by Brookshire *et al.* are erroneous.

Stevens *et al.* (1991) provide results of a CVM study designed to estimate the existence value of four species of wildlife. Their results, whilst lending support to the concept of existence value, illustrate the difficulty associated with its measurement. The majority of respondents in their study gave either protest responses (a refusal to answer in money terms) or unrealistically high bids given the level of their income.

According to Randall (1991) vicarious use value addresses the possibility that people who cannot visit unusual environments nevertheless gain pleasure from television or other media representations of them.

Notwithstanding these identification and measurement issues, Carson *et al.* (1992) provided a report to the Attorney General of the State of Alaska in which an estimate was given for the lost passive use (nonuse) value resulting from the Exxon Valdez oil spill. A median value of $31 per household in the USA resulted in a total damage estimate of $2.8Bn. Not surprisingly, Exxon-sponsored research under the supervision of Hausman (1993) has questioned the damage estimate of Carson *et al.* by focusing criticism on the very concept of nonuse value and on the legitimacy of CVM estimates in general. The bases of these criticisms are dealt with in Sections 3.5 and 3.7.

Attempting separate valuations of use and nonuse benefits or of policy subcomponents can cause serious problems in either overestimation or the obverse, underestimation through omission. However, Hoehn, Randall and Tolley in various papers (Hoehn and Randall (1982); Hoehn (1983); Randall, Hoehn and Tolley (1981); Randall (1991)) have concluded that piecewise sequential benefit estimation structures used for either policy subcomponent or total value component estimation can produce similar results to those given in the holistic context. The problem that does exist is that the values given to the subcomponents in a piecewise estimation are dependent upon their ordering in the valuation procedure. The total value may remain relatively constant but the values given to the subcomponents alter with their ordering. This, whilst not identical to Arrow's 'independence of irrelevant alternatives' discussed in Chapter 1, does bear some similarities.

Kahneman and Knetsch (1992a) refer to this as the embedding effect. These authors conducted experiments, and cite evidence from other studies, which support their hypothesis that the ordering of various levels of provision of some public good determine the valuations given. Their evidence, see Table 3.1, however, based on respondent's willingness to pay (WTP) for three levels of provision of Environmental Services can also be interpreted to support the hypothesis that respondents have a budget in mind which they are willing to devote to some form of Environmental Service. For instance, sub-sample, group 3, were offered only the option of contributing to 'Improved Rescue Equipment and Personnel' (a subset of 'Improved Disaster Preparedness' which in turn was a subset of 'Environmental Services'). If this sub-sample was given soley the option of contributing to a subset of the total 'Environmental Services' then it would appear invalid to draw the conclusion of an embedding effect. Rather, if some aspects of Environmental Services are denied to the respondents then it appears logical that they should allocate their budget where possible. Indeed, the mean WTP values across the three sub-samples are remarkably similar.

Table 3.1
Willingness to Pay for Selected Classes of Goods and Allocations of Totals to Less Inclusive Groups

		Sub-sample		
		Group 1 (N = 66) ($)	Group 2 (N = 78) ($)	Group 3 (N = 74) ($)
Public good				
Environmental Services	Mean	135.91		
	Median	50.00		
Improved disaster preparedness	Mean	29.06	151.60	
	Median	10.00	50.00	
Improved rescue equipment, personnel	Mean	14.12*	74.65**	122.64
	Median	1.00	16.00	25.00

* Two respondents did not answer this question, reducing N to 64.
** Four respondents did not answer this question, reducing N to 74.

Source: Kahneman and Knetsch (1992)

Loomis *et al.* (1993) also provide evidence which questions the findings of Kahneman and Knetsch. Using both open-ended and dichotomous choice (yes-no or take-it-or-leave-it) survey designs to estimate the value of forest protection in Southeastern Australia, Loomis *et al.* found that embedding effects were only apparent at one of the two levels tested. Where embedding did seem to take place, its effect was much smaller than that reported by Kahneman and Knetsch.

However, it should be noted that Loomis *et al.* did find some embedding and further work by Hoehn and Loomis (1993) does report significant benefit overstatement when consideration is given to two-program and three-program policies taken independently rather than as a whole. The overstatement was in the order of 24 percent and 54 percent respectively. These results are supported by the work of Wu (1993) although these findings suggest benefit overestimation of the order of twofold where policy subcomponents are estimated sequentially rather than as a whole.

The Kahneman and Knetsch (1992a) results are questioned by Smith (1992b) and Harrison (1992) whose reinterpretation of the design and implementation of the Kahneman-Knetsch CVM study suggests that a number of conclusions, including that given by the authors, could be inferred from the results. Smith uses this argument to dismiss the embedding problem although, whilst recognising some of Smith's criticisms, Kahneman and Knetsch (1992b) remain adamant that CVM estimates are prone to embedding effects. To dismiss this possibility, they argue, is to ignore one of the most serious potential drawbacks to the use of the CVM.

Kahneman and Knetsch (1992b) reiterate their suggestion that:

> The conservative conclusion from our findings is that future applications of CVM should incorporate an experimental control: the contingent valuation of any public good should routinely be supported by adequate evidence that the estimate is robust to manipulations of embedding. (p 91)

According to Nickerson (1993), whose critique of Harrison's (1992) results suggest that it is Harrison and not Kahneman and Knetsch who is in error, this would seem a reasonable request given the lack of definitive conclusions on the issue of embedding.

A further method of piecewise valuation is the piecewise independent valuation procedure discussed in Randall (1991) and here, it may even be the case that 'typical' values for subcomponents are used to build the total value (Sorg and Loomis 1984). Rather than using *de novo* estimates, shelf valuations are used. Hoehn and Randall (1989) and Randall (1991) have shown there to be problems in the accuracy of such a valuation procedure although the size and magnitude of the likely errors are unknown. The principal problem lies in the likely different substitutes and complements available for different characteristics in different locations. Table 3.4 and the associated discussion on benefit transfer in Section 3.6 provide evidence in support of the difficulty of building total values from typical subcomponent values. Often, there is no typical value, only a mean derived from a wide range of valuations.

The transferability of site specific valuation estimates into a piecewise independent valuation procedure is the principal issue which Smith (1992a) addresses. He concludes that users of the CVM must move forward from producing a body of literature consisting of diverse valuation case studies:

> to a more systematic set of benefit measures capable of being consistently aggregated or disaggregated. (p 25)

To achieve this goal, Smith argues that researchers in this field need to establish a standardised set of definitions of the environmental amenities and subsequently to develop a definitional structure to organise these commodities into classes. Randall's (1991) recognition of the problem of substitutability and complementarity between characteristics of a given location provide the main theoretical hurdles for future work in this area. A combination of the theory discussed in this chapter and in Chapter 4 is used as the basis of an attempt to provide transferability of the results given in Chapter 5.

The discussions in Sections 3.0 and 3.1 have led to the construction of a portfolio of requirements for a technique which could be used to enhance public participation. At this point, it is worth turning to the issue of how well the principal valuation techniques, currently employed in benefit estimation, perform against these requirements.

3.2 Indirect Valuation Techniques

Table 3.2 provides a useful categorisation of valuation techniques based on whether a person's behaviour is observed or hypothetical and whether the final valuation is gained directly or has to be inferred by the researcher.

Comparisons of results using various methods are dealt with in Section 3.5 under the heading of convergent validity.

Hedonic pricing and the travel cost approach are examples of observed indirect techniques whereas the CVM is a hypothetical direct technique.

The travel cost approach or Clawson technique, (Clawson (1959), Clawson and Knetsch (1966)), in its simplest form, estimates consumer's surplus for a particular amenity based on the cost of travelling, time costs and any admission fee. Willis and Garrod (1991) provide a recent example. In the zonal variant of the technique, contours are drawn around the amenity, each representing a distance zone. The average number of per capita visits to the amenity from residents of each distance zone is obtained usually via on-site questionnaire surveys and when combined with the cost of travelling, time costs and any admission fee, produces a demand curve for the amenity.

As a means of estimating total economic value this technique cannot be used alone as it fails to elicit the nonuse class of benefits discussed in the previous section. Further, a fundamental criticism centres on the inclusion of a value for time spent travelling to, or at, the amenity. Whilst it is theoretically correct to account for time spent in travel and on-site, assigning a value to it is somewhat arbitrary. Another difficulty associated with the use of the travel cost approach is that it is difficult to extricate single amenity (site) valuations from multi-site journeys. Also, the use value derived from observing actual travel behaviour does not show a maximum willingness to pay. For instance, someone may value an amenity so highly that they move house to be close by. Given an equivalent number of visits,

Table 3.2
Behaviour-based Methods of Valuing Public Goods

	Results obtained by observing valuations Directly[*]	Results obtained by observing valuations Indirectly[*]
Observed market behaviour	OBSERVED/DIRECT Referenda Simulated Markets Parallel private markets	OBSERVED/INDIRECT Household production (travel cost approach) Hedonic pricing Actions of bureaucrats or politicians
Responses to hypothetical markets	HYPOTHETICAL/DIRECT Contingent valuation Allocation game with tax refund Spend more-same-less survey question	HYPOTHETICAL/INDIRECT Contingent ranking Willingness-to-(behaviour) Allocation games Priority evaluation technique Conjoint analysis Indifference curve mapping

[*] The difference between the 'direct' and 'indirect' columns can be thought of, in the latter case, as the need to *infer* value from some behaviour. In the direct case, valuations are given *directly* by the respondent.

Source: Adapted from Mitchell and Carson (1989) p 75
(Travel cost approach made explicit)

the travel cost approach would now assign a lower value to the benefits derived by this individual than was the case before the relocation. Potential problems also arise in the choice of functional form and where there is multicollinearity between explanatory variables, especially among site environmental characteristic levels. As discussed in Chapter 1, this technique is also 'passive' in that respondents are not asked for their valuations directly, rather these are inferred from their travel behaviour patterns.

Hedonic pricing (Rosen (1974), Palmquist (1991)) the second of the observed-indirect methods in common useage, assumes that the price of a marketed good, (such as housing) is dependent on that good's characteristics (such as location, size, year of build and environmental amenities). Theoretically, by comparing data on house prices for which all variables, except the environmental good in question, are held constant, it would be possible to estimate willingness to pay for some quantity, (or quality), of the environmental good. In practice this is done using multiple regression analysis on cross-sectional data.

The principal problem with this technique is the exacting nature of the data required. Even though estate agents and mortgage companies have been willing to supply information, housing markets tend to be slow moving and true cross-sectional data is difficult to assimilate. Ensuring accurate data on subjective criteria such as neighbourhood characteristics is also difficult. A further problem lies in the need to estimate the effects of interactions between housing and labour markets. Where there is a poor environment for example, wages may rise to reflect this, thus artificially supporting house prices. In this instance, focus on house prices alone would tend to provide an underestimate of the cost of the poor environment. Some of the assumptions underpinning this technique also raise concerns. The most important is that individuals must be able to percieve environmental quality changes and that such changes would be accurately represented in house prices. Thus, the housing market must be competitive and individuals must have perfect information on (and understanding of) both house prices and environmental characteristics. This notion of perfect information is an overly restrictive assumption. Choice of functional form is a further area of potential problems for those seeking to use this technique and, where more than one aspect of, say, air quality is being studied, for instance, noise and particulates, it is very likely that multicollinearity will be present.

The hedonic pricing method, despite these criticisms, has seen significant use and praise as a benefit estimation technique. Smith and Huang (1993) have produced results of a meta-analysis of empirical studies which used hedonic pricing to value air quality. Their analysis of thirty-seven studies produced a list of some 167 separate estimates of the association between air pollution and property values. Standardising the results of these studies and the measurements of air quality enabled Smith and Huang to conclude that:

> Hedonic models can live up to the theoretical expectations developed for them. The available empirical literature does display a remarkably consistent pattern. (p 22)

However, as with the travel cost approach, hedonic pricing cannot estimate nonuse values. Valuation of amenities using this technique will thus provide underestimates of total economic value. Furthermore, and again like the travel cost approach, hedonic pricing does not seek 'active' participation from those who value an amenity. Although it could be argued that the actual travel to a site or the purchase of a house which provides certain levels of environmental characteristics is indeed active participation, this fails to show comprehension of the concept of involvement in decision making. Involvement requires that respondents are aware that they have an input to the decision-making process. In the use of either the travel cost approach or hedonic pricing this is clearly not the case. In fact, if either of the indirect methods were to be used, the full extent of consumer's surplus would need to be estimated which would entail the use of a hypothetical question to visitors or house purchasers seeking how far they would travel to a particular site or how much they would pay for a particular house, respectively. Both methods would then be classified as hypothetical-indirect methods which would command few, if any, benefits over the hypothetical-direct CVM but would retain many of their existing drawbacks.

This section has sought to introduce the two most commonly used indirect valuation methods, along with a brief description of the problems associated with their use. Neither is suitable for the job of enhancing the public participation process due to each being indirect or passive and that each only provides estimates of use value. Although both provide cardinal measures of welfare derived from particular amenities, and as they rely on actual behaviour the scope for strategic behaviour is reduced, neither technique lends itself to be used in the context of developing local plans. As such, the discussion of the indirect techniques is not extended here. Instead, the remainder of this chapter focuses on the CVM.

3.3 The Contingent Valuation Method - An Overview

The CVM is an example of a hypothetical-direct valuation technique requiring the active involvement of respondents (see Table 3.2). Where a policy change will bring about some environmental effect, those benefiting and those suffering a disbenefit are encouraged, via questionnaire surveys, to reveal their willingness to pay (WTP) for, or their willingness to pay to avoid, the policy change in question.[2] These values are summed for users and non-users alike and the net gains to society estimated. It will be argued in subsequent sections that careful use of the CVM can elicit both use and nonuse values for an amenity. In addition, the CVM focuses on *ex ante* (forecasted) behaviour before some change occurs whereas the travel cost and hedonic pricing methods, unless used in the context of benefit transfer, produce values *ex post*. Thus, estimates of changes in welfare of interest to the policymaker are theoretically better approached using the CVM than using the observed-indirect methods. Randall (1991) concludes that:

---

[2] Willingness to accept (WTA) (compensation) is also used although it will be shown in Section 3.4 that willingness to pay is, in most instances, the preferred method.

For now, there seem to be serious impediments to incorporating benefit measures based on revealed preference methods (hedonic pricing, travel cost) into a valid measure of *ex ante* total value. (p 317)

A further rationale for choosing the CVM over the revealed preference methods is its ability to estimate directly the substitution effect of a change in the quantity or quality of a public good. In the following section, this matter is discussed in some detail bringing together the two issues of measurement of welfare gain and the variation between willingness to pay and willingness to accept.

3.4 Measuring Consumer's Surplus

This section illustrates the trade-off inherent in the CVM. In one type of scenario for instance, respondents are required to state the maximum amount they would pay for a particular environmental improvement, say Q_0 to Q_1 in Figure 3.1. In the upper panel it can be seen that such a change, without any payment by the individual, would improve her or his level of wellbeing as shown by the move from A on U_0 to B on U_1. The CVM seeks to maintain the individual at the original level of wellbeing by requiring a respondent to state a payment equivalent to the vertical distance BC. Respondents thus state a hypothetical payment equal to the value they derive from the environmental improvement.

For a welfare gain: (letters in brackets refer to areas in Figure 3.1).

$WTP_{CpS}(c)$ < Marshallian Consumer Surplus (c+b) < WTA_{ES} (a+b+c)

and for a welfare loss:

$WTP_{ES}(c)$ < Marshallian Consumer Surplus (c+b) < WTA_{CpS} (a+b+c).

WTP - Willingness to pay CpS^3 - Compensating Surplus
WTA - Willingness to accept ES^4 - Equivalence Surplus

---

[3] CpS is theoretically correct in instances where the gain or loss *will* occur.

[4] ES is theoretically correct in instances where the gain or loss *will not* occur.

In this latter case, the individual is compensated for an increase not occurring, WTA_{ES}, or the individual pays to avoid a decrease, WTP_{ES}.

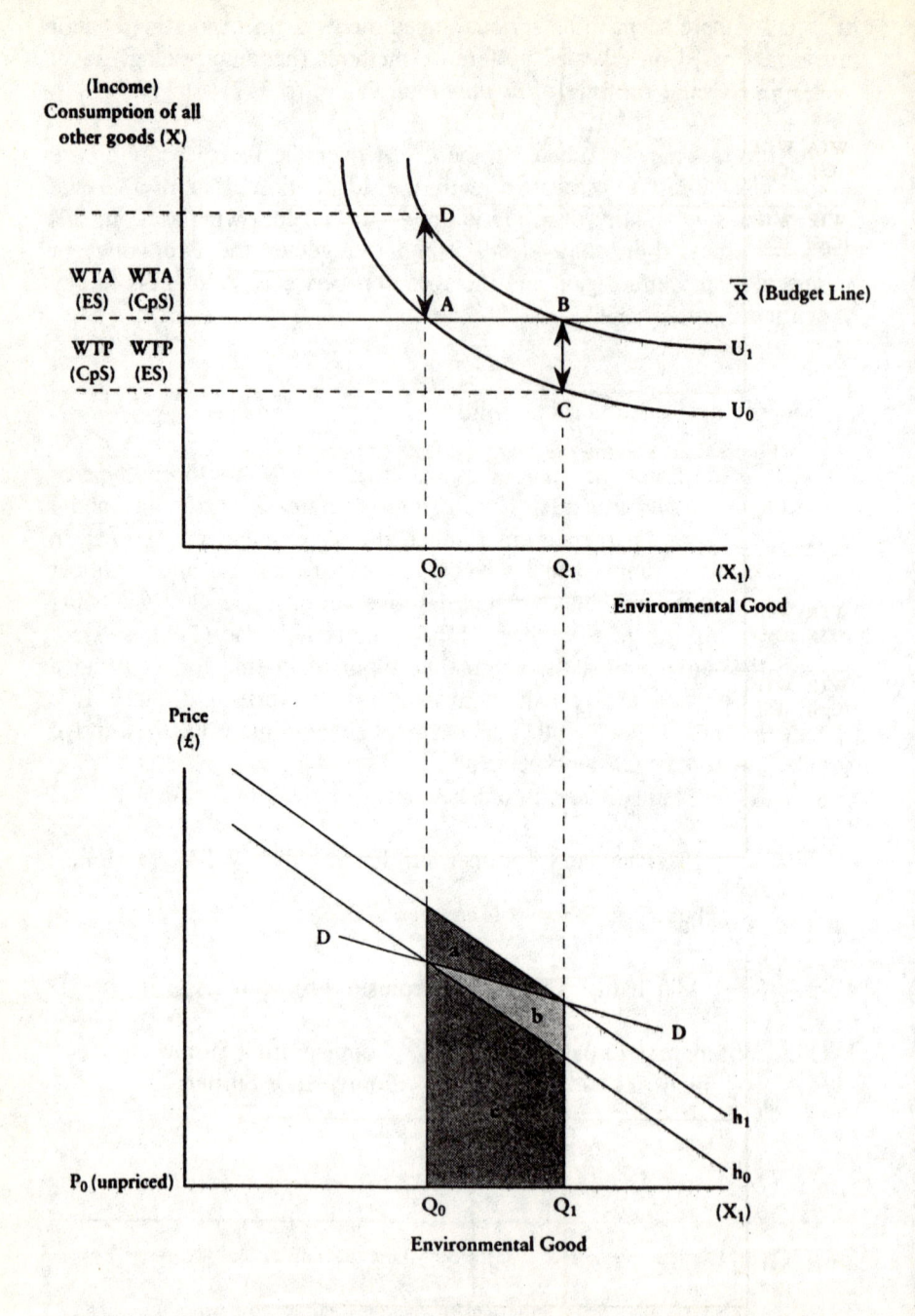

Figure 3.1: Compensating Measures of Welfare Gain and Loss for an Unpriced Quantity Constrained Environmental Good

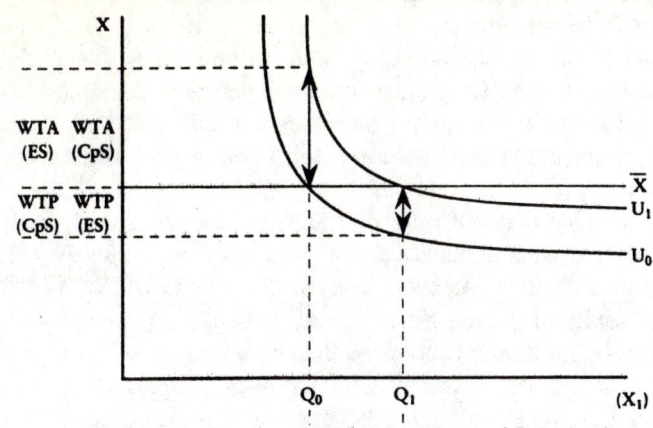

Figure 3.2: Varying the Marginal Rate of Substitution

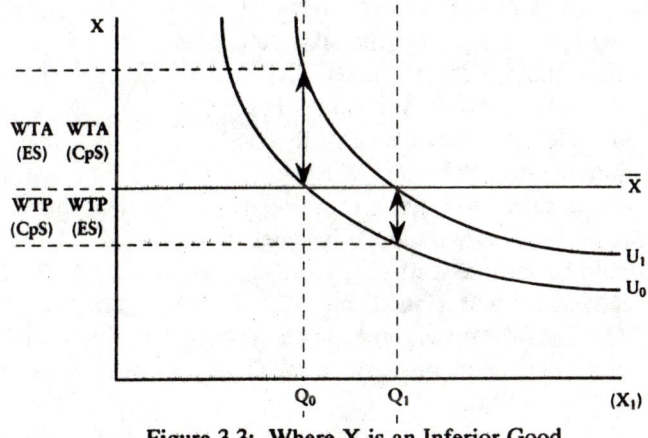

Figure 3.3: Where X is an Inferior Good

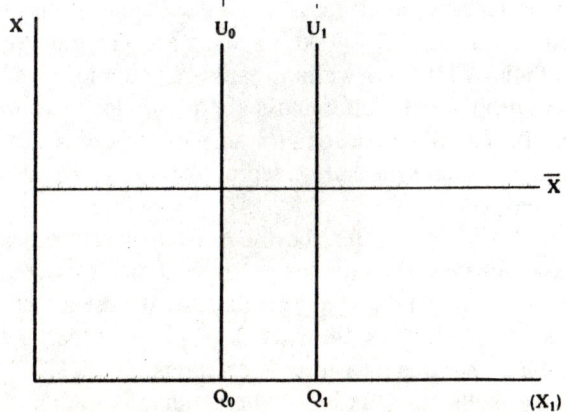

Figure 3.4: The Case of a Unique or Irreplaceable Environmental Good

For quantity or quality changes in an environmental good, the consumer's surplus measures can be read off the lower panel of Figure 3.1. DD is the Marshallian demand curve incorporating both income and substitution effects. The line h_0h_0 is the Hicksian income-compensated demand curve which leaves the consumer at the initial (lower) level of utility and h_1h_1 is the Hicksian income-compensated demand curve for a consumer entitled to the increased provision.

It is interesting to note that not only do the WTA measures include the area beneath the compensated demand curve at a higher level of utility, h_1h_1 in Figure 3.1, and therefore must be greater than the WTP measures, because of the convexity of the indifference curves the discrepancy between WTP and WTA can be far more pronounced than is suggested in Figure 3.1.

For a quantity, or quality, increase which moves a consumer from a relatively steep part of their indifference curve (a high marginal rate of substitution) to a relatively flat part of the curve (a relatively low marginal rate of substitution) the difference between WTP and WTA would be expected to be substantial. Figure 3.2 illustrates this point.

Furthermore, where the bundle of goods, (X), is seen as inferior, the indifference map will reflect this by the curves being tight together on the horizontal axis and wide apart on the vertical axis. This would tend to increase the variation between WTP and WTA, as shown in Figure 3.3.

Another possible scenario is reflected in Figure 3.4 which shows a consumer unwilling to accept any trade-off between goods X and X_1. Here the WTA value would be infinite justifying what may, by some, be seen as protest bids and is consistent with Hanemann's (1986; 1991) findings where the difference in WTP and WTA was shown to be dependent on the elasticity of substitution as well as on the income effect. WTP, in this case, would be bounded by the income constraint.

Returning to Figure 3.1, it is the Hicksian compensated demand curve that provides the theoretically correct measure of consumer's surplus for a change in the price or quantity of a good. The CVM, which by questioning respondents as to their WTP for a welfare gain (or to avoid a welfare loss) and WTA compensation for a welfare loss (or to forego a welfare gain), directly estimates the Hicksian consumer's surplus. This ability, for the CVM to estimate true welfare measures, represents an important advantage over the indirect methods.

Even though the CVM may offer the theoretically correct measures of welfare gain, (loss), debate still continues as to the choice between the WTP and WTA measures. Willig (1976) argues that the difference between the two measures may be small, as little as 2 per cent either side of the Marshallian consumer's surplus measure. Randall and Stoll (1980) managed to extend Willig's results to situations where quantity rather than price changed thus making the results more applicable to the valuation of many public goods. It was found by Randall and Stoll that where expenditure on the good in question accounted for a small amount of total personal income then the Marshallian and both Hicksian measures approximated each other with WTP and WTA being within 5 per cent of each other. At least, as Mitchell and Carson (1989) state:

> Considering the other possible sources of error in CV studies, differences of [the Willig - Randall - Stoll] magnitude between the WTP and the WTA formats are small indeed. (p 33)

Whilst these theoretical underpinnings of welfare measures were reassuring to researchers using the CVM, the empirical results of Hammack and Brown's (1974) study of waterfowl benefits reported WTA some four times greater than WTP amounts. Likewise, in a later series of large sample simulated market experiments, Bishop and Heberlein (1979; 1986), Bishop, Heberlein and Kealy (1983), and Knetsch and Sinden (1984), found large differences between WTP and WTA amounts. These empirical findings have been the source of much debate between researchers with suggestions for the large differences between WTP and WTA grouped in four themes. (The results presented in Chapter 5 of this work also illustrate large variations between WTP and WTA.)

First, Hanemann (1986) has demonstrated that the Randall and Stoll limit of WTP and WTA being within 5 per cent of each other is really dependent on two factors, namely the income elasticity for the environmental good and the elasticity of substitution between this and all other goods. Given that Houthakker and Taylor (1970) found that the upper limit on income elasticity rarely exceeded two, Hanemann was able to illustrate the sorts of values for the elasticity of substitution which would yield large differences between WTP and WTA. If the good in question had many close substitutes, and thus a large elasticity of substitution, the difference between WTP and WTA would be quite small. Where the converse is true, as is the case with many unique or irreplaceable environmental goods, WTA could, theoretically, differ significantly from WTP amounts. In fact in a later paper, Hanemann (1991) proves that in the case of a unique environmental good (or loss of life) WTP would be the individual's entire (finite) income while WTA could be infinite. This is consistent with the diagrammatic representation provided in Figure 3.4.

Secondly, in Section 3.1 environmental goods were seen to give rise to both use and nonuse values. Sen (1967) and Turner (1988) have argued that individuals possess both private and public preferences giving rise to different valuation processes when comparing free environmental goods with marketed private goods. The existence value element of total economic value is thus suggested as a cause of WTP differing from WTA amounts.

The WTA concept suggests that the present generation could be compensated for the loss of some amenity whereas if the individual does have some existence value (perhaps a desire to leave the amenity for a future generation) then the WTA question may meet with some resistance. It may feel immoral to be compensated for the next generation's benefits. This may result in a refusal to answer the WTA question or in inflated responses. The WTP question on the other hand, if worded correctly, can, theoretically, elicit the values given to the subcomponents of total economic value and should not, for the reason outlined here, result in protest responses.

Similarly, respondents may not accept that they have the right to sell the environmental good resulting in a rejection of the implicit property rights in WTA question formats. This again could lead to protest responses and substantial differences between WTP and WTA.

A third proposition put forward to explain the divergence between WTP and WTA is based on the fact that market prices are the outcome of consumer's repeated evaluations of goods whereas values obtained using the CVM are one-off valuations often with significant potential consequences if, say, the amenity is totally removed. Respondents are unlikely to have had previous experience in valuing public goods in money terms, especially in a culture like that of the UK relative to that of the USA, and are therefore likely to be cautious. Hoehn and Randall (1982) have suggested that in such circumstances risk aversion will tend to lead to overestimation of the compensation required, WTA, and underestimation of WTP. This is suggested by Coursey *et al.* (1987) and by Singh (1991) who found that repeated CVM trials for a public good led to declining WTA figures as the respondents became more familiar with the evaluation process. Both Coursey *et al.* and Singh also reported that WTP amounts did not alter significantly with the repeated trials suggesting that WTP was quite an accurate initial estimator of the value of the good.

Fourthly, Mitchell and Carson (1989) have argued that prospect theory as developed by Kahneman and Tversky (1979), Tversky and Kahneman (1981), may also provide an explanation for the divergence of WTP and WTA. Mitchell and Carson contrast prospect theory with standard utility theory. The latter suggests that equivalent increments and decrements from some initial position should yield the same values. Using prospect theory they argue that it is possible to show that the value function for losses is steeper than that for gains thus resulting in the divergence between WTP and WTA. However, using the argument of a diminishing marginal utility derived from consumption of the environmental good it is also possible to arrive at the asymmetrical total value curve depicted in Figure 3.5.

In Figure 3.5, the individual has an initial endowment of the public good Q^o. Equivalent increments and decrements to be valued take the individual to Q^+ and Q^- respectively. Reading off the total value curve it can be seen that WTA > WTP. The convexity of the indifference curves in Figure 3.1, is determined by the diminishing marginal utility of consumption of the two goods. This alone would suggest a total value curve of the same shape as that shown in Figure 3.5. According to Knetsch (1989; 1992) it is also theoretically possible that the total value curve would become kinked at $Q^°$ due to some feeling that the existing level of provision is 'right'. This would lead to an even greater divergence between WTP and WTA.

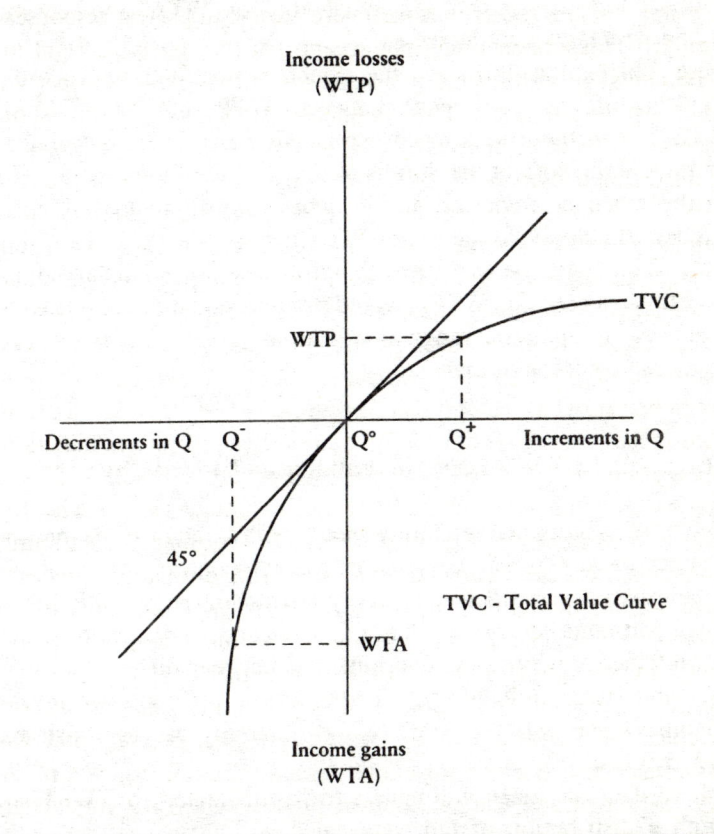

Figure 3.5: Asymmetrical Total Value Curve showing WTP/WTA Variation

Knetsch (1989) provides evidence from three experiments which illustrates the divergence between WTP and WTA. His results suggest that the endowment effect produces nonreversible indifference curves with losses being more highly valued than equivalent gains. These results include both experiments where income effects were likely and those involving relatively small sums of money leading to very small expected income effects. The conclusion of nonreversibility holds for both sets of experiments. In one of the experiments, for instance, respondents were given an initial endowment of either of two goods. When asked if they would exchange their endowment for the other good, 89 percent of those with good A refused to swap for good B and 90 percent of those with good B refused to swap for good A. Knetsch (1992) reports similar results of nonreversibility.

McDaniels (1992) also provides evidence of the disparity between WTP and WTA. In a study with regard to safety features in a near market, hypothetical new vehicle purchase, it was found that the choice of the reference point determined the WTP for, or WTA compensation for, equivalent increases and decreases.

These four explanations, and the evidence presented by Knetsch and by McDaniels, of the divergence between WTP and WTA cause some consternation to those seeking to use the CVM. Where a welfare gain is under review the correct measure is WTP_{CpS}. (See Figure 3.1). However, given the evidence reviewed above, where a welfare loss is considered, researchers should avoid the use of WTA measures and, instead, should use WTP_{ES}. The latter measure reveals willingness to pay to avoid a welfare loss. Estimates based on WTP_{ES} would provide valuations towards the lower bounded end of a possible range of valuations. Such conservatism may also be appealing to decision makers.

3.5 Error and CVM - Issues of Validity and Reliability

The issues of validity and reliability should both be addressed when assessing the results of any research. In the present context, for example, it is important to consider whether a survey instrument is estimating the correct Hicksian consumer's surplus values (validity) and, furthermore, whether the values obtained are consistent over time and between different samples taken at the same time (reliability). Errors cause problems of invalidity or unreliability. The issues of validity and reliability can be illustrated using Figures 3.6 and 3.7.

If there is a true mean willingness to pay indicated by TWTP in Figure 3.6 with a distribution of bids, (revealed willingness to pay, RWTP) as shown by the solid line, any error which leaves the distribution unchanged but shifts the estimated mean in either direction will produce invalid results. In the CVM, starting point bias (see Section 3.7.2.2) would be one example.

To illustrate the concept of reliability, again consider a true mean willingness to pay indicated by TWTP in Figure 3.7 with the distribution of bids shown by the solid line. Any error which leaves the mean unchanged but increases the variance of the bids would lead to unreliability. By chance, if this were the case, samples drawn from a population with a large variance may report widely differing mean WTP bids.

Probability density
function of RWTP

TWTP   Willingness to pay

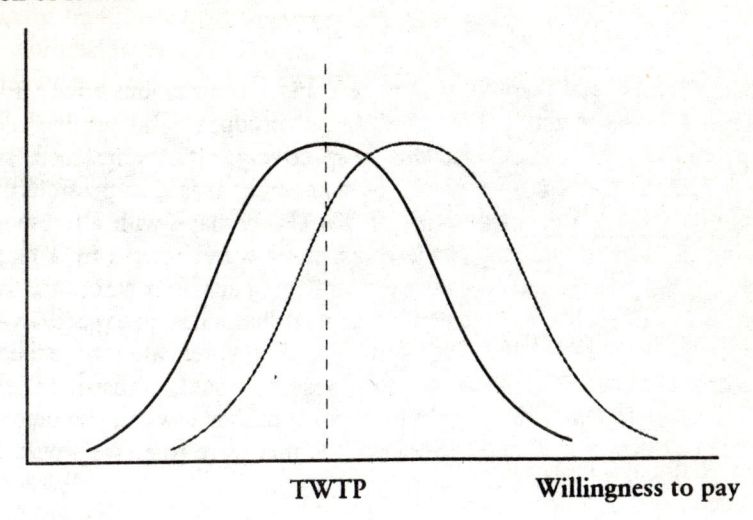

Figure 3.6: Validity

Probability density
function of RWTP

TWTP   Willingness to pay

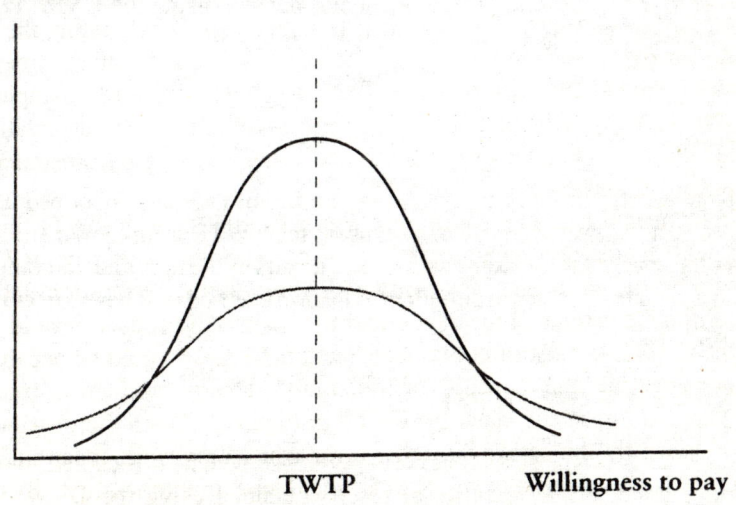

Figure 3.7: Reliability

The issues of validity and reliability can also be illustrated using a standard linear equation:

$$RWTP = \alpha + \beta TWTP + \epsilon \qquad (3.1)$$

where α and β are unknown parameters and ϵ is a random error term with expected value of zero. For the CVM to produce valid results, α and β must take the values zero and one, respectively. If, for instance, starting point bias were to exist, α would be non-zero. It is also possible that the bias could be related to the size of TWTP, perhaps with all respondents giving inflated responses. If these responses were inflated by a factor of, say, 100%, perhaps due to consistent strategic behaviour across the sample, then β would equal 2. Whilst it is assumed that ϵ has an expected value of zero, the variance of the error term could, theoretically, be expected to increase with the size of TWTP. Respondents would, perhaps, be less able to reveal their TWTP for a gain/loss which pushes towards the outer limits of their ability to pay and vice versa. If this were true, we would have a case of increasing heteroscedasticity.

Let
$$Var(\epsilon) = \sigma^2 TWTP^{\gamma} \qquad (3.2)$$

In Equation (3.2), if there were a proportional increase in Var (ϵ) as TWTP increased, then it would follow that $\gamma = 1$. If it were hypothezised that the variance increased more than proportionately then $\gamma > 1$. If either hypothesis were accepted, var(ϵ) would increase as TWTP increased, causing problems with the reliability of estimates derived using the CVM. The case of perfect reliability would be when Var (ϵ) = 0.

3.5.1 Validity

It is inherently difficult to assess the validity of estimates obtained using the CVM. In the vast majority of instances, the TWTP is unknown and tests for bias must rely on an examination of the survey design and in comparisons with estimates derived from other valuation methods. These are considered in turn.

3.5.1.1 Construct Validity

Kahneman and Knetsch (1992) offer evidence which, if accepted, would cast serious doubt on the validity of results obtained using the CVM. In their experiments they found a high positive correlation between 'moral satisfaction' gained from, and WTP for, a public good. From this scanty evidence, bearing in mind that correlations show little other than the existence of a relationship between two variables, these authors conclude that where WTP is given by a respondent, it is WTP for moral satisfaction rather than for the public good in question. Their evidence however would not seem strong enough to support their conclusion as moral satisfaction is likely to be a determinant of WTP for a public good and, as such, would be expected to be correlated with WTP. Moral satisfaction may even be the basis of some existence values as discussed in Section 3.1.

The principal problem in demonstrating the construct validity of the CVM is, as stated above, that there is rarely a TWTP value to be observed. (If TWTP could be observed with ease, there would be little point in using the CVM!). In order to test the underlying theory, (construct validity), it is necessary to examine the theoretical basis of RWTP to see if it is likely to be a good estimator of TWTP. It is worth noting that even in instances where money values, (TWTP), can be observed against which the RWTP can be compared, by so doing, the researcher is implicity assuming that actual money sales accurately reflect Hicksian consumer's surplus. As an example of the literature suggesting that this might not be the case, a study by Pratt, Wise and Zeckhauser (1979) reported the ratio of prices of the same commodities across different stores in the same city varying between 1.11 and 6.67. According to Smith (1992b), these results question the correctness of using Hicksian consumer's surplus as a measure of welfare change. However, if it is accepted that RWTP can be used as a proxy for Hicksian consumer's surplus, and that Hicksian consumer's surplus is the correct measure, then it only remains to expand the theoretical underpinning of RWTP in order to examine the CVM for construct validity.

The CVM approach relies upon the theoretical foundations implicit in the Fishbein-Ajzen (1975) attitude-behaviour model.

Figure 3.8 gives a diagrammatic representation of the Fishbein-Ajzen model. In CVM studies, specified behaviour or the final action (actual payment or compensation), rarely occurs. The revealed willingness to pay question measures 'intention to perform specified behaviour'. This is based on bipolar attitudes towards that behaviour such as good/bad or strong/weak and on the 'subjective norm' which represents pressures to comply in some way exerted by relevant persons such as friends, relations or work colleagues. The latter, 'subjective norm', is the balance of the 'ought to', 'ought not to' thoughts that are held by the individual and concerning the action. The former, 'attitudes', are determined by the informational base acquired by the individual with regard to the action and its consequences.

The model is useful in so much as it allows researchers using the CVM to elicit instances where overstatement of WTP is likely to occur. For instance, where the beliefs of a respondent suggest, erroneously, that the change in question would result in positive knock-on effects on other goods, the RWTP for a change may overstate the TWTP ($\alpha > 1$ in equation 3.1). Likewise, because the TWTP for a change may be contextually based, perhaps depending on the perceived state of the economy, it is important that the framing of the questionnaire depicts a similar state of the economy to all respondents. (Information requirements are dealt with in Section 3.7.2.1.)

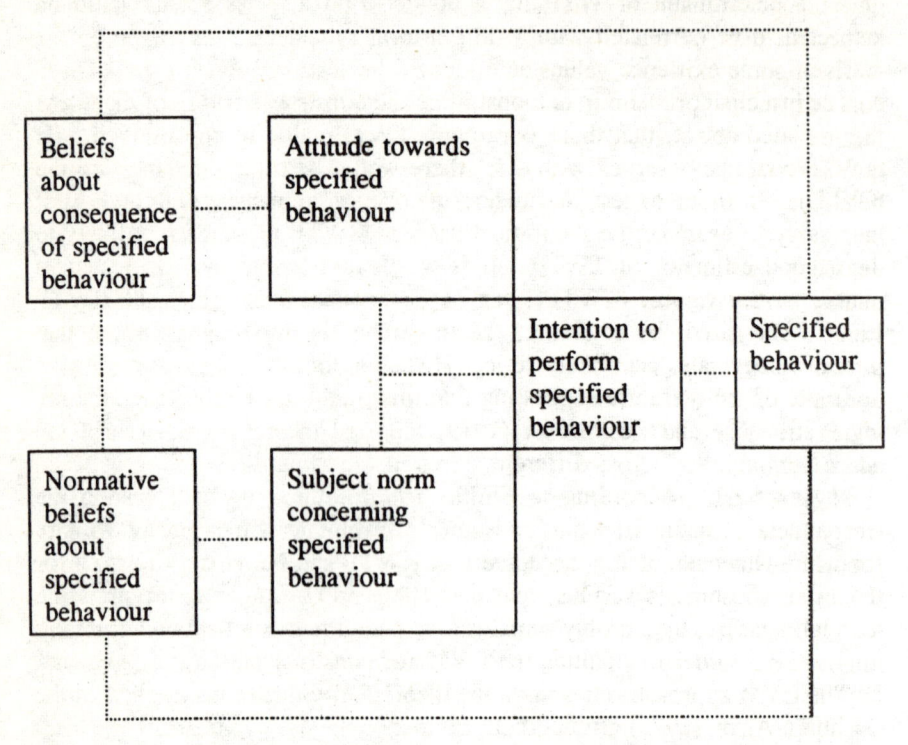

```
┌─────────────┐     ┌─────────────┐
│ Beliefs     │     │ Attitude    │
│ about       │─────│ towards     │
│ consequence │     │ specified   │
│ of specified│     │ behaviour   │
│ behaviour   │     │             │
└─────────────┘     └─────────────┘
                          │
                    ┌─────────────┐     ┌─────────────┐
                    │ Intention to│     │ Specified   │
                    │ perform     │─────│ behaviour   │
                    │ specified   │     │             │
                    │ behaviour   │     │             │
                    └─────────────┘     └─────────────┘
                          │
┌─────────────┐     ┌─────────────┐
│ Normative   │     │ Subject norm│
│ beliefs     │─────│ concerning  │
│ about       │     │ specified   │
│ specified   │     │ behaviour   │
│ behaviour   │     │             │
└─────────────┘     └─────────────┘
```

Figure 3.8   Fishbein-Ajzen Model for Predicting Specific Intentions
Source: Fishbein and Ajzen (1975)

Fishbein and Ajzen were able to develop three hypotheses which can be considered when evaluating a particular survey instrument. The first of these, *correspondence*, refers to the likely correlation between the question asked and the intended inference to be drawn from the answer. For example, if the inference to be drawn from questioning a respondent is whether or not she is likely to visit a specific park, asking her about her attitude to open spaces may give an indication of internal consistency of the questionnaire but it is unlikely to yield good forecasts of her visiting the park. Correspondence is defined to include the comprehensiveness of the question asked in terms of the specific action, upon whom or what the consequences of the action will fall and the context (including the timing) of the action.

The second hypothesis, *proximity*, refers to the stage within the Fishbein-Ajzen model to which the question is addressed. The proximity hypothesis states that the closer the stage addressed is to the behavioural intention stage, the better the answer given will be as a predictor of actual behaviour. Questions concerning attitudes are more likely to yield good predictions of behaviour than are questions focusing on the belief stage.

The third hypothesis, termed *familiarity*, is the one which causes most concern in the CVM context. Fishbein and Ajzen suggest that the more familiar a respondent is with the behaviour in question, the more useful questions relating to attitude or behavioural intention are in predicting actual behaviour. In the CVM context, actual behaviour is TWTP whereas behavioural intention may be seen as RWTP. In most circumstances, a high degree of familiarisation with the consequences of changes in the quantity or quality of environmental goods is unlikely. Use of the feedback loop in Figure 3.8 is therefore severely limited and must be enhanced in the interview situation by giving an adequate amount of relevant, useful and unbiased information. Familiarisation with the payment mechanism and the wider issue of giving monetary values for nonmarketed goods should also be addressed.

Boyle *et al.* (1993) tested whether question ordering and familiarity (respondent experience) played a part in a respondent's willingness to pay for white-water boating in the Grand Canyon. Their findings suggest that the importance of question ordering declines as the degree of familiarity with the hypothetical change increases. These findings have important implications for the design of a survey instrument where a respondent's familiarity with the focus of the research is low. Similarly, Davis and O'Neill (1992) found that a lack of familiarity with the hypothetical scenario led to problems with the reliability of responses.

However, conflicting evidence is provided by Kealy *et al.* (1990) who found that familiarity had little influence on the reliability or validity of estimates obtained using the CVM. Instead, these authors conclude that the CVM design and especially the respondent's belief in an explicit payment obligation would be more important for high intention-behaviour consistency.

Where these three hypotheses are incorporated into the CVM design, the RWTP will be a closer approximation of TWTP, and therefore also a closer approximation of the Hicksian consumer's surplus measure, suggesting a higher probability of achieving valid and reliable results.

Closely related to construct validity is content validity, tests for which are used to examine how well the actual survey design addresses the underlying construct developed by the researcher. Do the questions posed in a survey adequately address that which is being sought by conducting the survey? By not including some information which has been theoretically identified as being an important determinant of TWTP then, depending on its relationship with TWTP, this may lead to invalid results if the mean bid shifts or unreliable results if the variance of the bids increases.

The relevance for the CVM researcher lies in the questionnaire design. Pilot testing of questions, and of information supplied to respondents, should be conducted in order to identify ambiguities and omissions. Furthermore, where a total economic value is required, pre-tested questions should be addressed to both user and nonuser samples.

3.5.1.2 Predictive Validity

As Friedman (1953) stated, the most valuable test of a model is its predictive capability. The problem for those using the CVM is again the fact that only rarely are observed values available for comparison. Predictions of actual behaviour through WTP questioning for environmental goods can rarely be compared with actual behaviour itself. Whilst it is therefore virtually impossible to test predictive validity in such a context, it is, however, possible to examine the predictive validity of the CVM in other (market) contexts. Where such tests for predictive validity of the CVM in the market context do yield good results, reference to the Fishbein-Ajzen model suggests that such results should not be extrapolated to the environmental goods case. The issue of 'familiarity', that is knowledge and experience of the good, of the consequences of the proposed change, of the payment mechanism and of giving monetary valuations for environmental goods, may not be as strong as in the market situation.

Various studies (Bohm (1972); Bishop and Heberlein (1979); Kealy *et al.* (1988); Dickie *et al.* 1987)) using the CVM and subsequent actual sales figures have been conducted and although, for the reasons given above, there is a reluctance to accept their conclusions as evidence of the predictive validity of the CVM in the environmental context, it is recognised that such tests do not disprove the hypothesis that RWTP = TWTP. Furthermore, where actual sales and RWTP do not closely correspond, the Fishbein-Ajzen model suggests that this may simply be due to new information being received by the respondent between the time of interview and actual purchase. It can be argued therefore that if predictive tests for validity give poor results it may not be due to a problem with the CVM at all. It seems then that such tests for predictive validity will be of limited use in providing a theoretical underpinning for the CVM.

3.5.1.3 Convergent Validity

Convergent and predictive tests of validity vary, principally, due to the timing of the samples taken. Predictive tests must, by definition, occur in two different time periods. Tests for convergence on the other hand should, where possible, run concurrently with the CVM survey.

Convergence tests seek to validate the CVM by comparing the values for RWTP with valuations obtained for the same environmental good using different methods of valuation. The principal methods which have been used for comparison are the travel cost method and the hedonic price method although Shechter (1991) has also provided comparisons using, amongst others, health production techniques.

As discussed in Section 3.1 and in O'Doherty (1993), both the travel cost and hedonic pricing methods of valuation have been shown to be limited when considering measurement of total economic value (use and nonuse values) and therefore tests for convergence between CVM results and those obtained using the travel cost and or hedonic pricing methods should be treated with some caution. Notwithstanding this criticism, CVM researchers have conducted such tests for convergent validity and in general, have reported reasonably strong convergence for the CVM and one, or both, of the other valuation methods. Cummings, Brookshire and Schulze (1986) in their 'State of the Arts Assessment' report the results of eight tests of convergent validity using the CVM and either of the two methods, travel cost or hedonic pricing. All comparisons were within 60 percent of each other.

Given that the travel cost approach cannot measure nonuse values, it is not surprising to find that estimates from CVM studies are generally higher than those found using the alternative method. However, in a study by Loomis et al. (1991), 90 percent confidence intervals for the estimates derived using both the CVM and the travel cost approach were found to overlap although, as anticipated, the mean from the travel cost approach was lower than that derived using the CVM ($119 and $183 respectively).

Tests of convergent validity can also be conducted between different designs of CVM surveys. Different payment mechanisms for instance can be given to two sub-samples of the population. Kealy et al. (1988) used such a test and found no significant difference in RWTP using open-ended and dichotomous-choice type formats. In a more recent study, Shechter (1991), compared the results from the CVM with those of three other valuation methodologies; preference, health production and cost of illness. In the same study, sub-samples within the CVM sample were given different payment mechanisms. His results, shown in Table 3.3, suggest a reasonable level of convergent validity both between the CVM and preference and health production techniques and between payment mechanisms within the CVM. The concurrent nature of the test for convergent validity is important in order that variables such as preferences and income can be considered to be stable.

Smith (1992b) has also reviewed the convergent validity of the CVM against damage functions and against models of mitigation decisions. In the former, Smith is sceptical about the results because of the subjective judgment necessary in, for instance, defining 'restricted activity days' to describe a health effect. Smith is also critical of using mitigation decisions, arguing that there are serious limitations in what households recall about their expenditures and about the benefits accruing from those expenditures. Smith also questions the usefulness of comparing estimates from the CVM with those derived using hedonic models. He argues that:

> ... the methods do *not* measure the same concept of benefits and would not perform equally well in capturing all the benefits realized by respondents ... (p 14)

Table 3.3
Comparisons between Direct and Indirect Valuations of a 50% Change in Perceived Pollution Levels[1]

	WTP_{CpS}	WTP_{ES}
	Mean annual sum per household in Israeli currency (NIS)	
CVM		
Open Ended	37.7	70.9
Modified Iterative Bidding	67.8	89.0
Binary Choice	66.2	69.1
Indirect		
Preference Model	9.83[3]	73.3
Health Production	90.0[2]	
Cost of Illness (bed days)	185.0	

1. Including true zero bids.
2. Including spouses and children
3. The text of Shechter's paper suggests that due to a problem in his definition of air quality, this result may be ignored.

Source: Shechter (1991)

Furthermore, Smith identifies the case where comparisons are made between the CVM eliciting annual payments and hedonic models which use actual prices for homes as assets. Providing an annualisation of the change in asset value requires the researcher to assume how an individual perceives the discount rate and the time horizon involved in the contract.

3.5.1.4 Divergent Validity

Tests of divergent validity assess whether different valuations are given for different goods by the same population using the same survey design and preferably within the same time period. Theoretically, if a particular methodology is valid for measuring one type of amenity then its application to a different amenity, *ceteris paribus*, should result in different valuations being obtained. (This is of course only correct if the valuations between the two goods are truly different). Very few tests of divergent validity have been reported although given the number of studies undertaken using the CVM in recent years, it would be relatively easy to compare their results. This would, of course, be treating the results as if taken from a split sample rather than from the same sample as would be preferred. An examination of Table 3.4, which details the ranges of estimates derived from valuations of various activities, would tend to suggest that tests of divergence are of little interest in assessing the validity of the CVM. For divergence to be a useful concept, tests of convergence must also be accepted and the extremely wide range of valuations for the same activities illustrated in Table 3.4 do not suggest a high degree of convergence.

3.5.2 Reliability

According to Reiling *et al.* (1990) relatively few tests have been developed and conducted in order to measure the reliability of CVM survey results when compared to those intended to measure the validity of the method. In fact, they state that, by 1990, only six such studies could be found, *viz*; Heberlein (1986); Jones-Lee *et al.* (1985); Kealey *et al.* (1988); Loehman and De (1982); Loomis (1989); and Musser *et al.* (1988).

Loomis (1989) states that the reliability of the CVM requires that two conditions be met. Firstly, if TWTP has not changed over time then the valuation given for an amenity by a respondent should also remain unchanged. The second condition states that where TWTP has changed, then this change should be reflected in RWTP. In the vast majority of cases using the CVM, the TWTP will be unknown and therefore changes would not be identifiable. The Fishbein-Ajzen (1975) model again offers the researcher a framework from which the determinants of willingness to pay can be hypothesised. Changes in variables, such as income, over the relevant period would tend to support the hypothesis that $TWTP_{i0} \neq TWTP_{i1}$, where i indicates a particular respondent and the subscripts 0 and 1 are two time periods. This sampling at different times is referred to in the literature as the test-retest situation. Whilst references to studies concerning reliability tend to focus on this situation, another test of the reliability of estimates from the CVM is an examination of the internal consistency of a particular respondent's answers.

Internal consistency can be tested by incorporating essentially the same question in different formats at different stages of the interview. Although this appears theoretically easy, in practice respondents may recognise the second question as a rerun of the first and answer accordingly. Where this occurs and is not detected, reports of reliability will be overstated.

The test-retest reliability checks are also useful for another purpose. The test-retest, where it does give close, intertemporal valuations for the same environmental good, provides the decision maker with greater confidence in the 'shelf-life' of the survey results. The 'shelf-life' of survey results will be a major determinant in the practicality of benefit transfer, discussed in Section 3.6 which focuses on the construction of transferable demand functions for use in a piecewise independent valuation procedure.

Loomis (1989) argues that reliability is a necessary condition of validity on the grounds that whilst reliable answers may be biased in a particular direction, reliability does indicate consistency and that the method is picking-up a 'substantial deterministic component of respondent's behaviour' (p 77). Loomis attempts to test the hypothesis proposed by Cummings *et al.* (1986) that:

$$H_o: V(t_o) = V(t_1)$$

where $V(t_o)$ is the value given in time period zero for some environmental good and using a specific CVM design and $V(t_1)$ is the value given (preferably by the same respondent) in time period one for the same good and using the same design. Using the condition stated above and rewriting the hypothesis in terms of WTP, we get:

$$RWTP_{i0} = RWTP_{i1}$$

where, again, subscript i refers to a particular respondent and the subscripts 0 and 1 refer to two time periods. This condition should hold if there has been no change in TWTP over the periods.

Where CVM studies only report means, test-retest results will overstate the reliability of the method. For example, if two individuals, A and B, gave valuations in time period 0 and 1 of £60 and £40 respectively the mean would be £50. The same mean would be arrived at by A and B reversing their valuations and by focusing solely on the mean, the reliability of the method would be overstated. In reality, there would have been a significant change in valuation given by both respondents. A better test to perform would involve pair-wise comparison of each individual's valuations over time.

Reiling *et al.* (1990) recognise the practical problem that respondents involved in retest interviews may be influenced by the previous interview to respond in a certain way, and that in cases where respondents are able to recall their initial valuation, the subsequent valuation will tend towards this figure. In addressing this problem, Reiling *et al.* propose that the same survey design should be administered to two distinct samples at different points in time. They argue that if the population characteristics are unchanged between the two time periods then the RWTP should remain largely unchanged. This test could also be used to indicate the likely accuracy of benefit transfer. However, as stated above, split half samples would not allow for pair-wise comparison and by using only sample means, reliability would tend to be overstated.

The study by Reiling *et al.* was concerned with the potential variability of RWTP due to seasonality factors. They conclude that:

> Estimated contingent values are reliable and do not vary significantly with the timing of the survey. (p 132)

A similar, positive, finding is the outcome of the study by Loomis (1989) who used the test-retest procedure to conclude that:

> .... the test-retest results in this paper support the contention that the contingent valuation method provides reliable estimates of total willingness to pay..... (p 83)

The Loomis study was conducted with a nine month interval between test and retest and the author is careful to point out the dangers of extrapolating the conclusion of reliability beyond this timescale. This study also tested for reliability in the two categories of benefits, use and nonuse. A general household survey was conducted alongside a survey applied to visitors to the amenity in question, Mono Lake in the USA. The positive conclusion of reliability applied to each benefit category.

Before considering some of the potential sources of error in the use of the CVM, and as the tests of reliability also relate to tests of benefit transfer, it is appropriate to consider the practice of benefit transfer at this point. The focus on the CVM is returned to in Section 3.7 where the sources of error in CVM surveys are considered.

3.6 Benefit Transfer - An Overview

Benefit transfer (BT) is the developing practice of using valuations based on primary data gathered at 'study' sites to estimate potential changes in consumer's surplus at a proposed 'policy' site. In the context of this research, BT would be used as a cost-effective mechanism for gauging the intensity of feeling of a relevant population to proposed changes in a local plan.

Interestingly, BT, although only now provoking so much interest in the literature, has been employed for many years. Many researchers are now questioning its validity but, as Opaluch and Mazzotta (1992) illustrate, these are, ironically, the very same people for whom BT has been second nature for many years. Opaluch and Mazzotta suggest that BT occurs by simply extrapolating from a sample to statements about a population in a site-specific valuation study. However, apart from some pioneering work by Sorg and Loomis (1984), it is only relatively recently that site-specific valuations from study sites have been used to estimate changes in consumer's surplus at policy sites. It is this extension of the scope of BT which has provoked much debate.

BT has been used in various other contexts for many years. Brookshire and Neill (1992) trace the historical background of the practice of BT and, in so doing, identify three stages in its development. Insofar as the BT used in each of these three stages is still practised, the three stages can also be seen as three methods of BT. The first method represents estimates based upon expert opinion, the second, estimates based on observed behaviour and the third, estimates based on preference-elicitation techniques. Brookshire and Neill (along with Walsh *et al.* (1992) and Boyle and Bergstrom (1992)) suggest that the practice of BT based on expert opinion of unit-day values for recreational facilities has, lamentably, been used in the USA for over 25 years. In less obvious instances BT, if only in terms of implied shadow prices, has, and still is, used globally in decisions as commonplace as the choice of, for example, road safety schemes. These authors claim that the procedures used in BT to this date have lacked any scientific basis and they align this practice to that employed in litigation cases where compensation is determined by *ad hoc* expert opinion.

As valuation techniques were developed and refined, observed behaviour based valuations, to some extent, superseded expert opinion in BT and, in turn, preference-elicitation methods are now challenging as the basis for BT.

Section 3.6.1 details the sources of demand for BT, focusing on factors which are leading to an increase in that demand along with constraints on the number of new valuation studies being undertaken. In Section 3.6.2, various approaches to BT are discussed.

3.6.1 The Demand for Benefit Transfers

The demand for BT is a derived demand, although in the area of litigations discussed below, the causal relationship is unclear.

The demand for BT is derived from the demand for valuation studies, which has been given impetus, especially at the federal level in the USA, by Executive Order 12291. As outlined by Smith (1984), federal bodies such as, although not exclusively, the Environmental Protection Agency (EPA) were charged with using cost-benefit analysis to assess policy. This same impetus to the demand for valuations has not been formally manifest in the UK although, in areas such as the planning context of this research, where it is suggested that the existing procedures of local government would be enhanced by employing valuation techniques, the implications are similar to the American context. The increasing demand for valuations by local government is acknowledged by McConnell (1992) who states:

> One example of this realisation is the emergence of the no-growth/ antidevelopment movement, which is spurred in part by the nonmarket costs of growth. Benefit analysis, because of its focus on nonmarket activities, can play an important role in this area. And especially here the transfer of benefits will be attractive, because it is unlikely that governments at this level will be interested in funding full-scale benefit studies. (p 695)

The third impetus to the increasing demand for valuation studies comes from the legal profession, again predominantly in the USA, which increasingly bases claims for compensation on nonmarket valuations. It is unclear, however, if the rise in demand for BT has been due to exogenous factors, such as an increasing incidence of environmental damage, or whether the development of BT has reduced potential costs for claimants and thus increased the demand for BT-based valuations.

Overall, the increasing demand for nonmarket valuations has coincided with the increasing imposition of a number of constraints on those who would seek to satisfy the demand by undertaking new studies. The principal constraints relate, firstly, to the short time horizons for decision makers reliant on benefit estimates and, secondly, to a reducing financial resource base for undertaking primary studies at policy sites. Increasing demand and, given the above constraints, a reduced supply, have led to the search for alternative methods of estimating benefits. The outcome has been the increasing focus on the validity and reliability of BT.

Desvousges *et al.* (1992b) have presented this problem more formally as:

$$\text{Minimise MSE } (\hat{o}) = \text{Var } (\hat{o}) + (\text{Bias } (\hat{o}))^2 \qquad (3.3)$$
Subject to: $AF = AF^0$ and $AT = AT^0$,

where AF and AT are available funds and available time, respectively, and MSE represents the mean square error of the benefit estimate, $\hat{o}$. The bias element of the constrained optimisation set out in Equation (3.3) addresses the validity of the estimate; can $\hat{o}$ be expected to measure the 'true' benefit? The variance component refers to the reliability of the estimates.

Where the benefit estimate is substantially larger than the costs of an associated proposed policy, the need to scrutinise the variance and bias is reduced and, at the extreme, negated. However, where the outcome of the cost-benefit analysis is less clear cut, it is important to establish objectives for the required accuracy of any BT.

Required Accuracy

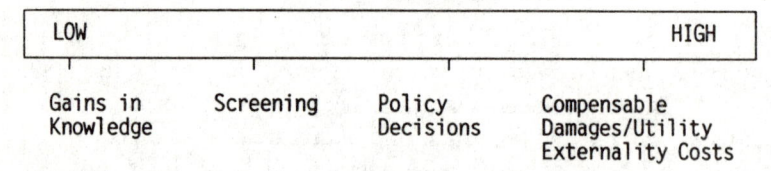

```
|LOW                                                     HIGH|
 |              |              |              |
 Gains in       Screening      Policy         Compensable
 Knowledge                     Decisions      Damages/Utility
                                              Externality Costs
```

Figure 3.9: **Continuum of Decision Settings from Least Required Accuracy to Most Required Accuracy**
Source: Brookshire (1992) p 6

Brookshire (1992) recommends that the final use of the benefit estimate be the determining factor in its required accuracy and he proposes a spectrum of required accuracy for BT which is reproduced in Figure 3.9.

Deck and Chestnut (1992) and Brookshire and Neill (1992) also adopt this decision-context framework for assessing the required accuracy of BT. Deck and Chestnut suggest that the appropriate criterion should be the possibility of adopting a wrong decision by using BT. Brookshire and Neill recommend that BT be used only towards the 'low' end of the continuum.

Desvousges *et al.* (1992a) also offer a continuum similar to that shown in Figure 3.9, although they seem to be more optimistic about the potential for BT. The focus of their reseasrch is on the use of BT in the Natural Resource Damage Assessment (NRDA) procedures in the USA. These procedures would be located towards the "compensable damages" in Figure 3.9. Their continuum (see Figure 3.10) runs from initial screening assessment of damages through to litigation, and their recommendation is that BT should play an important role in both screening assessment and in negotiated settlements.

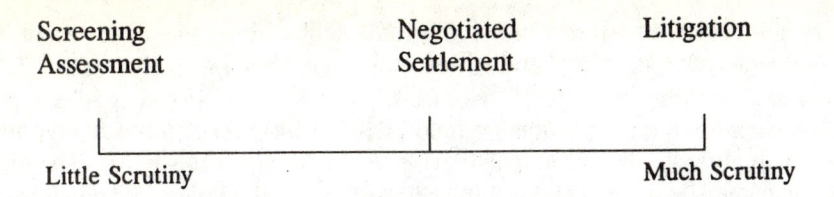

```
Screening                Negotiated              Litigation
Assessment               Settlement
        |_____|_____|
Little Scrutiny                                  Much Scrutiny
```

Figure 3.10: Continuum of Valuation Scrutiny in an NRDA Context
Source: Desvousges et al. (1992a) p 7

These settlements are typically Type A assessments which deal with small, short-duration, marine and coastal pollution spills. Using data on a relatively few key variables, a (loss of) benefit estimate is generated based on a simple BT model which is calculated using knowledge from previous experiences of the effects from similar spills. The authors are careful to state that, where litigation is likely, BT of this sort is unlikely to be defensible in the courts.

It appears that the recommended use of BT depends both on the required accuracy of the benefit estimate and upon the standpoint (or optimism) of the researchers. Figure 3.11 illustrates this point.

The low and high on the 'Degree of Optimism...' scale correspond to the two camps identified among researchers by Smith (1992a). Smith suggests that many economists fall into one of two camps when the concept of BT is on the agenda: those who see merit in waiting for the ideal data and those who believe that some information is better than none. These groups can also be allied to the 'idealists' and 'pragmatists' identified by Boyle and Bergstrom (1992).

		Required Accuracy/Scrutiny	
		LOW	HIGH
Degree of Optimism in the use of BT	LOW	Unsure, possibly tempered use	Don't use
	HIGH	Use	Tempered use

Figure 3.11: Likely Recommended Use of BT: By Researcher's Optimism and Required Accuracy

Where the objective is one of 'gains in knowledge' (Figure 3.9) as it is in the experiments reported in Chapter 5, there are also important implications for the choice of sample size. Given this objective, and tight resource constraints, the sample size for this work was kept relatively small. Of course, if the objective was to lie towards the "compensable damages" end of Brookshire's spectrum, the sample size would need to be adjusted accordingly.

This section has highlighted the determinants of increased demand for benefit estimation, along with an outline of the financial and time constraints which are imposed on researchers. The outcome of such a constrained optimisation has been an increasing focus on the use of BT. Whilst, from Figure 3.11, it can be seen that not *all* researchers in *all* instances would recommend the practice of BT, it is also apparent that *some* researchers in *some* instances would view BT as a useful tool for satisfying both research and legislative needs.

In the planning context of this research, it is likely that BT would prove useful. From the evidence presented in Chapter 2, it would seem that little or no benefit estimation is undertaken in the development of local plans, and the resource implications for Local Authorities of conducting original studies in each instance would undoubtedly deter its implementation. By implication, the current required accuracy for benefit estimation in local planning is low. The likely recommendations for the use of BT are then, at least initially, tempered use or full use. The following section outlines a number of approaches to BT and details a number of criteria which should be met in order to achieve defensible benefit estimates using BT.

3.6.2 Approaches to Benefit Transfer

There are a number of methods of generating benefit estimates using BT. First, and by far the easiest, but potentially the most inaccurate, is to take a mean value obtained for some activity at a study site and to transfer this to the policy site. Examples of this method, based on 'Net Economic Values per Recreation Day' by type of activity undertaken, are given by Sorg and Loomis (1984) and in an updated version of their work by Walsh *et al.* (1992). A summary of the latter is given in Table 3.4. A number of problems with this method are apparent from inspection of the table. The median values for all activities are lower than the associated mean values, suggesting that a small number of large values may be influencing these results. Furthermore, the range of values in certain activity categories is unacceptably high. For example, the range for "Boating, nonmotorised" is from $10.26 to $183.36 and even the 95% confidence interval for this same category stretches from $17.61 to $79.75. The reporting of a mean value $48.68 to two decimal places must be considered spurious and the use of this mean value in BT could be grossly misleading. This criticism applies, *mutatis mutandis*, to the majority of the other activity categories.

Table 3.4
Net Economic Values per Recreation Day Reported by Travel Cost and Contingent Valuation Demand Studies from 1968 to 1988, Unites States (third quarter 1987 dollars)

Activity	Number of Estimates	Mean	Median	Standard Error of the Mean	95% Confidence Interval	Range
Total	287	$33.95	$27.02	$1.67	$30.68-37.22	$3.91-219.65
Camping	18	19.50	18.92	2.03	15.52-23.48	8.26-34.89
Picnicking	7	17.33	12.82	5.08	7.37-27.29	7.05-46.69
Swimming	11	22.97	18.60	3.79	15.54-30.40	7.05-42.94
Sightseeing and off-road driving	6	20.29	19.72	3.73	12.98-27.60	10.33-31.84
Boating, Motorized	5	31.56	25.67	10.36	11.25-51.87	8.27-68.65
Boating, nonmotorized	11	48.68	25.36	15.85	17.61-79.75	10.26-183.36
Hiking	6	29.08	23.62	5.82	17.67-40.49	15.71-55.81
Wintersports	12	28.50	24.39	4.48	19.72-37.28	11.27-66.69
Resorts, cabins, and organized camps[a]	2	12.48				3.91-19.93
Big game hunting	56	45.47	37.87	3.47	38.67-52.27	19.81-142.40
Small game hunting	10	30.82	27.48	3.51	23.94-37.70	18.72-52.04
Migratory waterfowl hunting	17	35.64	25.27	5.87	24.13-47.15	16.58-102.88
Cold Water Fishing	39	30.62	28.49	3.24	24.27-36.97	10.07-118.12
Anadromous Fishing[b]	9	54.01	46.24	11.01	32.43-75.59	16.85-127.26
Warm Water Fishing	23	23.55	22.50	2.46	18.73-28.87	8.13-59.42
Salt Water Fishing	17	72.49	53.35	14.05	44.95-100.03	18.69-219.65
Nonconsumptive fish and wildlife	14	22.20	20.49	2.30	17.69-26.71	5.27-38.06
Wilderness	15	24.58	19.26	6.10	12.62-36.54	8.72-106.26
Other recreation activities	9	18.82	16.06	3.65	11.67-25.97	6.81-43.39

[a] Resorts were 1.83% valued at $19.93 per day; seasonal and year-around cabins were 3.06% valued at $3.91 per day; and organized camps were 1.79% valued the same as camping.
[b] Anadromous fishing estimates included in cold water fishing. Estimated as roughly 5%.

Source: Walsh et al. (1992)

To some extent, Walsh *et al.* accept these criticisms and suggest that the extreme range of values may be caused by the socio-economic characteristics of users, the quality of the activity site or by the valuation methods used in the original studies. By way of improvement, they suggest that:

> A potentially useful approach to the benefit transfer problem would be to pool the data from existing studies and apply multiple regression analysis. If the basic model specification is complete, that is, if it includes the relevant explanatory variables in the correct functional form, then it could explain the variation in benefits embodied in differences amongst the explanatory variables. The net benefit estimated for a site lacking data would then be predicted by inserting appropriate values of explanatory variables into the model fitted to data from other study sites. (p 707)

In implementing this suggested improvement, estimating *adjusted* mean unit values, Walsh *et al.* used a number of dummy variables and proxies to represent characteristics inherent in the original studies, *viz* valuation method, type of payment question used (if CVM), location of survey (on-site or off-site), quality of site and socio-economic characteristics. Using this adjusted method, they found that around 40% of the variation in benefit estimates could be explained by their model. However, whilst this adjusted mean unit value method gives an improved basis for BT, the large amount of unexplained variation in valuations still exists.

Smith (1992a), Smith and Huang (1993; 1995) and Smith and Kaoru (1990) have developed a similar approach to that detailed above. Their 'meta-analysis' approach uses benefit estimates from previous studies, along with details of the methods used in the valuation, the means of measurement of an externality and the method of estimating socio-economic characteristics. In effect, meta-analysis uses historical data collected from a range of sources and attempts to identify causal relationships between explanatory variables and benefit estimates. The principal problem lies in the fact that the original studies were never designed to be pooled in this way and, as such, the onus is on the analyst to standardize variables such as quality of the good, quality of the study, quality of substitutes and to find proxies for socio-economic variables of the sample where these are not given in the original study. Smith (1992a) acknowledges the many problems associated with meta-analysis and suggests that many questions need to be answered in order to establish this technique as a reliable basis for BT. These questions include:

(1) What criteria should be used to compare the sample of 'comparable' studies?
(2) What measure should be used to summarize estimates across studies: consumer surplus, elasticities, etc?

(3) Can these summaries be used for benefit estimates as part of the transfer process?
(4) Should studies be weighted based on their 'quality' (ie considering the research procedures, data etc)?
(5) Can estimates from completely different modelling strategies such as travel cost demand models, random utility models, and hedonic travel cost be combined?
(6) Can estimates from indirect methods be pooled with contingent valuation results?
(7) How should the multiple models applied to a common data base, as is frequently reported in applications, be incorporated in a meta-analytic data base?
(8) How should the estimation uncertainty inherent in each study's estimates be incorporated in these analyses? (Smith (1992a) p 692).

It is interesting to map the development of the adjusted mean unit values and the meta-analytic approaches as platforms for BT. These methods are now verging on, and may well have initiated, the most recent method of BT, the transfer of demand functions. Although the results of Hanley and Ruffell (1993) would suggest otherwise, it is likely that the characteristics of the site being valued, and those of the relevant population, are major determinants in benefit estimation. The emergence of BT based on the adoption of demand functions from previous studies explicitly requires that data on the major determinants of valuations be included. This inclusion is not dissimilar to that suggested by Smith (1992a) and Boyle and Bergstrom (1992) for the direction of future BT research and has been the stumbling block for those attempting to use past studies not designed for the purpose of BT.

Boyle and Bergstrom (1992) state that site attributes and population socio-economic characteristics are key determinants in valuation. The demand function for a specific site may then be expressed as:

$$v_i = f(X, C_i, S) \tag{3.4}$$

where the valuation given by individual i, v_i, is a function of site attributes, X, socio-economic characteristics, C_i, and the price (availability) of substitutes, S. Boyle and Bergstrom suggest that BT would be most accurate where the study site and policy site have similar attributes and populations. This may be true in the early stages of applying this technique as the number of point estimates relating to explanatory variables, such as site attributes, would be relatively small. However, as the number of studies increases, giving rise to many estimates for different attribute vectors, the functional form of the relationship between valuation and explanatory variable would become more evident. The analyst involved in BT would then calculate the appropriate value given the quantity (or quality) of each of the relevant explanatory variables at the policy site.

A speedier route to establishing the form of the relationships between dependent and explanatory variables over a wide range of quantities (or qualities) could be achieved by using multiple responses from the same respondent. This would entail employing the factorial survey design method (see Chapter 4), together with the CVM. The results from, and shortcomings of, such an application are discussed in Chapter 5.

Bergland *et al.* (1995) have recently completed what they claim to be the first study designed solely to assess the reliability and accuracy of BT. In their study, they compared both the benefit estimates and benefit functions at two similar sites with similar populations given a proposed improvement in water quality. Whilst they conclude that their basic hypothesis of transferability of estimated per household benefits could not be rejected, the result in relation to the transferability of the benefit function was less promising. They conclude that their study casts 'serious doubt about the potential of transferring benefit functions across sites'.

Strangely, practitioners of contingent valuation have overlooked the fact that some early tests of the reliability of benefit estimates could also be interpreted as assessing the accuracy of BT. Given that the transferable demand function approach to BT relies, in the developmental stages at least, on study and policy site having similar physical and population characteristics, the split half sample tests of reliability actually use identical physical and population characteristics. Thus, where mean or median estimates and the benefit function across the two samples are acceptably similar, BT could also be deemed to have worked. The test-retest method (using different samples from the same population) of assessing the temporal reliability of contingent valuation estimates (Reiling *et al.* 1990), also provides an indication of the accuracy of BT and of its durability over time.

3.6.3 A Summary of Benefit Transfer

Given that the demand for benefit estimates is increasing, along with ever tighter resource constraints, thereby reducing the likelihood of funding for original studies, the focus of attention for many pragmatic researchers in this field has turned towards BT.

BT has been shown to be most acceptable in cases where required accuracy is toward the 'low' end of the decision-setting spectrum (Brookshire (1992)), where the objective is to secure 'gains in knowledge' (see Figure 3.9). This is exactly the objective in this work where, in these early stages of introducing benefit estimation into the public participation process of local planning, it seems appropriate to establish the technique in this context before using any results in actual policy decisions. Deliberations at this stage also focused on legitimising the use of a relatively small sample size in the experiment reported in Chapter 5. This was substantiated by stating that the objective for the research was one of gaining knowledge about the application of the technique in a planning context, rather than seeking results for use in actual policy.

A number of approaches to BT have been established although, as these techniques have been developed and refined, the distinctions between them have become blurred. Mean values for a 'recreation activity day' have been improved by adjustments for site quality and socio-economic characteristics. Meta-analysis, which draws on the results from a large number of studies in order to achieve a transferable benefit estimate, has suffered from the lack of uniformity, and thus comparability, across original studies. These developments have culminated in the transfer of whole demand functions from study sites to policy sites. However, until a large enough database is established, only proposed policies where the effects are likely to be similar to those at similar study sites with similar population characteristics could be estimated. A speedier route to establishing a large database, whole functional forms of relationships rather than point estimates, was suggested. This would involve the use of factorial survey design, reviewed in Chapter 4, along with the CVM. Although a large sample size would be preferred on statistical grounds, a less accurate but significantly cheaper route would be to use multiple responses from a limited number of repondents. This latter route is adopted given that the aim of the experiments reported in Chapter 5 is to estimate solely the likely potential for enhancing the public participation process in a planning context rather than producing useable, policy-relevant figures at this stage.

In the preceding sections of this chapter, consideration has been given to the best way in which the intensity of feeling of members of the public could be captured. Given the requirement to use cardinal, rather than ordinal, measures of preference, and furthermore, that these should be money-based, economic valuation techniques were reviewed along with the categories which must be estimated. The CVM was found to be the most appropriate technique although implementing this as part of all public participation exercises would be expensive. A low cost solution to this problem would involve the use of BT although this is likely to reduce the accuracy of preference estimation. However, it is not just in employing BT that may lead to error, the CVM itself has some potential pitfalls. These are reviewed in the next section.

3.7 Sources of Error in CVM Surveys

Errors in the design, sampling or execution stages of a CVM survey may result in invalid or unreliable estimates of TWTP. Where the error increases the variance of RWTP it affects the reliability of the survey results but does not lead to invalid estimations. If the error causes results to shift in a particular direction, this would cause problems in the validity of the results, (in Equation 3.1, $\alpha \neq 0$). Where the error is in someway proportional to the TWTP, $\beta \neq 1$ in Equation (3.1) and again, the results would be invalid.

Unreliable estimates would be manifest in the case of random variation in the error term, between either split half-samples or test-retest samples. According to Mitchell and Carson (1989) the variance of RWTP is due to two factors: a deterministic component which reflects the true variance in TWTP and also the random error component. The latter can be controlled to some extent by the researcher in the choice of sample size and by careful use of survey design and execution. Any part of the questionnaire which is ambiguous, or if a scenario is unrealistic, would result in guesses rather than informed valuations, increasing the variance and therefore reducing the reliability of the survey results.

Where an unexpected factor, such as the framing of a particular question, is found to increase the variance of the error term it is possible that, by conducting further studies, that factor can be controlled or at least its implications incorporated into the analysis of the results. For example, a choice of payment mechanism may have resulted in variations in RWTP which at first appeared to be random. Further study and experimentation, however, may have given researchers the confidence to state the direction and, perhaps, the size of the problem. What was initially considered as a reliability problem becomes one which, potentially, produces invalid results which could be adjusted correctly.

Rowe, d'Arge and Brookshire (1980) have argued that where possible, payment mechanisms and other sources of error should be neutralised in their effect on the results. However, Arrow (1986), Kahneman (1986), Randall (1986) and Mitchell and Carson (1989) reach a different conclusion. Where a particular payment vehicle is being used in a survey of a change to some environmental good, they argue that respondents do not value the change in the good in isolation of the wider policy context and, they conclude, the correct measure of value is the one which includes attitudes towards (and therefore valuation of) the payment vehicle as part of the wider policy.

Issues relating to the problems caused by error can be categorised according to whether the associated error is respondent or researcher based. Each of these categories is dealt with in turn. Although many of the sources of error raised here overlap both categories, such a split is useful for ease of exposition.

3.7.1 Respondent-Based Sources of Error

Although there are many potential sources of error which may be attributed to respondents, the two of principal concern are the potential for, and likelihood of, respondents acting strategically and whether respondents can deal with the hypothetical nature of the CVM. Unlike any problems caused by the hypothetical nature of the CVM, strategic behaviour would be a conscious act by respondents.

3.7.1.1 Strategic Behaviour

In Chapter 1, one of the problems encountered with existing voting and preference revelation mechanisms was identified as the potential for respondents to engage in strategic behaviour. Here, the CVM is analysed in the light of this potential problem and the ways by which CVM researchers attempt to design out the problem are reviewed.

Strategic behaviour by individuals might be thought to falsify the results of CVM surveys as individuals either overestimate or underestimate their RWTP in a hope to either secure the provision of a good or to enjoy the good at a low price (if provision is assured).

Whilst strategic behaviour may lead to stated valuations (RWTP) departing from TWTP, it is also possible that respondents want to be seen to give 'sensible' answers and by picking up clues in the course of the interview, give values approximating to the mean. Either of these behavioural patterns may lead to unreliable or invalid estimates of TWTP.

Mitchell and Carson (1989) suggest that the tendency towards strategic behaviour is dependent upon the perceived payment obligation and perceived probability of provision of the good. This is illustrated in Table 3.5. Using this framework it is possible to examine the relevance of behaviours TP, SB_{1-4} and ME to CVM researchers.[5] The different behaviours depicted rest on the assumption that the respondent has a positive value for the good in question. Where negative or zero valuations exist for TWTP, a different framework would need to be established.

TP is irrelevant to most CVM studies because of the absence of markets and SB_3 is said to be irrelevant due to the difficulty in conveying the impression that respondents would have to actually pay their RWTP. Furthermore, CVM instruments should not be worded in such a way that suggests provision of the good is likely regardless of RWTP again providing

---

[5] TP, SB_{1-4} and ME are all forms of strategic behaviour which respondents may engage in during the interview. See Table 3.5 for an expansion of these abbreviations.

further evidence that SB_3 is unlikely to occur and likewise suggesting that behaviours SB_4 and ME are improbable in the CVM context.

Table 3.5
A Priori **Expectations of Strategic Behaviour in CV Settings**

	Obligation to pay perceived as:		
	Amount Offered	Uncertain Amount	Fixed Amount
	Provision of good perceived as contingent on revealed preferences(RWTP)		
Motivation	True preference(TP) revelation	Variable(SB_1)	Overpledge(SB_2)
Direction	True value	Uncertain	Overbid
Strength	Strong	Weak to moderate	Strong
	Provision of good perceived as likely, regardless of revealed preferences(RWTP)		
Motivation	Free Ride(SB_3)	Free Ride(SB_4)	Nonstrategic Minimise effort(ME)
Direction	Underbid	Underbid	Random
Strength	Strong	Weak to moderate	Moderate

Source: Mitchell and Carson (1989) p 144

SB_2, with a strong motivation to overbid, is caused by the respondent perceiving that RWTP will determine provision of the good but where TWTP will bear no relation to actual payment levels. This behaviour can be designed out of CVM surveys by conveying to the respondent the impression that the actual amount to be paid is uncertain but provision of the good is still dependent on RWTP.

Such design considerations in alleviating worries about the other types of strategic behaviour do force the respondent into behavioural group SB_1. In this situation, the researcher is unsure of the direction and strength of the strategic behaviour although Mitchell and Carson conclude that the motivation to engage in such behaviour will be weak due to the following factors (p 155).

1. The informational requirements for strategic behaviour are great (and not costless).

2. CVM surveys normally convey to respondents the impression that a large number of people are being interviewed. The perceived likelihood that overpledging by a *credible* amount will affect the outcome significantly, when it is averaged over a large number of people, is low.

3. Most of the payment vehicles customarily used in CVM studies, such as taxes, higher prices, or higher electricity bills appear to invoke strong budget constraints and other negative reactions. People do not lightly pledge to increase these kinds of payment, even in hypothetical situations.

4. Underpledging carries the risk that the public good will not be provided, as CVM surveys normally present as a choice a situation in which provision is credibly uncertain.
    (Mitchell and Carson (1989) p155, emphasis in the original, parenthesis added[6])

Rowe *et al.* (1980), Brookshire *et al.* (1976), and Bohm (1984) have conducted various tests for strategic behaviour although these are flawed by their inability to separate strategic behaviour from other sources of error. All three on the other hand find little evidence of any error at all suggesting the results are free from the hypothesised strategic bias.

For example, the test by Brookshire *et al.* examined the distribution of RWTP. If strategic behaviour was present, they argue, then the results should consist of many 'outlier' responses. (Respondents giving zero or just credibly high bids). The problem here is one of excluding those who gave honest zero bids, these being bids from respondents who have zero income or no preference or negative preference for the good. The need to remove these outliers is however questioned by Smith (1980) who suggests that the majority of respondents will be free riders engaging in small undervaluations

---

[6] There does appear to be a contradiction in Mitchell and Carson's argument with regard to point 2 above. They appear to advocate (p 130) that a small sample size is preferred in order to avoid the strategic behaviour categorized as ME in Table 3.5.

with a few anti-free riders compensating with large overvaluations. He suggests, although offers no evidence in support, that there is little effect on the mean RWTP. Reliability may be lowered but the results should, he argues, remain valid.

Whilst some researchers have followed the path of testing for strategic behaviour, others have sought to examine the theoretical basis of the free-rider syndrome. Clarke (1971) and Groves (1973) have proposed incentive-compatible demand revelation devices (ICDRDs) in which a respondent's RWTP is actually the 'selfish' strategy. Green and Lafont (1978) consider implementing the ICDRD approach by indicating to respondents that they are part of a small sample which will be taken to represent the views of the relevant population. This information, they argue, would provide respondents with the incentive to aquire and consider information about a proposed policy in order to give an informed reply rather than an ill-considered one. The incentive mechanism here, implying to respondents that their input to some decision process will have a significant affect on the outcome, should not be taken as justification for using a small sample size. Indeed, Green and Lafont suggest that the optimum sample size, n, is proportional to the size of the relevant population, N, and is given as $\sqrt{N}$. Whilst this appears to be at variance with traditional sampling theory which suggests that the sample size be determined independently of the population size, in this public good case the total cost of a wrong decision being taken is dependent upon the number of people affected. Thus, Mitchell and Carson's comment with regard to sample size (point 2 above) should be treated with some caution as there are benefits to be derived from small samples such as the likely reduction in coalition forming due to the difficulty in identifying others in the sample. The conflicting recommendations from Mitchell and Carson and Green and Lafont appear to hinge on the difference in what respondents are told about the sample size and the actual sample size used in the survey. Respondents should be made to believe that they are part of a small sample whereas the researcher should adopt a different, larger, sample size in the conduct of the survey.

Among those who have examined the theoretical basis of the free rider syndrome are McMillan (1979), Evans and Harris (1982) and Watson (1991). Their findings support the hypothesis that co-operative rather than selfish behaviour would be pursued where the dynamic gains from co-operation outweigh the static gains from free riding. This conclusion is analogous to the outcomes where cartels operate in oligopolistic market structures. These conclusions support the notion that little, if any, free riding would take place by respondents in well designed CVM surveys.

A form of strategic behaviour could be manifest where self-selection takes place in a mail CVM survey. Whitehead (1991) estimated that aggregate benefits in mail surveys could be upwardly biased by as much as 50 percent due to this problem. Where mail surveys are used, therefore, the recommendation must be that a face-to-face interview control sample run concurrently.

3.7.1.2 The Hypothetical Nature of the CVM

The issue of whether behaviour in hypothetical markets can approximate to that in real payment markets, could equally be addressed here under respondent-based sources of error or in the subsequent subsection under researcher-based sources of error. It will be shown that informational issues are linked to the hypothetical nature of the methodology but in so much as these are problems for the researcher at the design stage, these are dealt with in subsection 3.7.2.1. Here, the theoretical issue of how respondents cope with the hypothetical situation in a CVM survey is addressed.

The first argument used to support the hypothesis that respondents can and do cope with hypothetical situations uses hypothetical simulated market experiments to compare results of RWTP against subsequent actual payments in a simulated market. Bohm (1972), Bishop et al. (1983) and Bishop and Heberlein (1986) have attempted to compare the RWTP amounts against actual payments made for semi-public goods. The latter two studies were conducted in the USA where, it might be argued, the hypothetical question of paying for public goods is not as anathema as it may be to those in the UK or from other cultures where provision of public goods is seen as more of a right of the individual. The conclusions from these studies are a point of debate in the literature with Bohm, for instance, stating that, in the hypothetical situation, respondents would act 'irresponsibly' due to the lack of real incentives to do otherwise. Mitchell and Carson (1989), however, in a reworking of Bohm's results, and by removing some outlier responses, find RWTP and actual payments to be quite similar. Other tests of the impact of the hypothetical nature of the CVM have been conducted using actual voting behaviour as a measure of the convergent validity of CVM studies, (Carson, et al. (1986)). Such referenda tests, although not comparing RWTP with TWTP, do provide strong support for the argument that behavioural intentions in a hypothetical situation do closely correspond to actual voting behaviour at a later date. Indeed, this result is especially important in the context of this work where the CVM is being assessed as a means of extending a simple voting referendum to a cardinal-based referendum mechanism. As a valuation technique, the CVM is undoubtedly a cardinal measure and it appears from Carson's results that the CVM does produce a similar outcome in terms of direction of voting intention to that obtained in simple voting exercises.

Further evidence supporting the argument that respondents are able to cope with the hypothetical nature of the CVM focuses on the Fishbein and Ajzen (1975) attitude-behaviour model (discussed in Section 3.5) where it was concluded that if the issues of correspondence, proximity and familiarity were addressed, then the potential problems relating to the hypothetical nature of the CVM would be reduced.

Whilst these arguments lend support for the view that the hypothetical nature of CVM may be either irrelevant or 'designed out', perhaps even more convincing is the massive spend on market research both in product testing and consumer valuations of these products, often with little previous consumer experience of the category of product. If market research did not work, it would not be employed. The issue of error due to the hypothetical nature of the CVM moved Carson (1991) to conclude that:

> .... even though the hypothetical nature of the situation may increase the variance of the responses and may make the responses more susceptible to other potentially biasing influences, no evidence exist from WTP studies to suggest a systematic direction for the results of a hypothetical as opposed to a simulated market. (p 140)

This suggests that the hypothetical nature of CVM may cause a problem with the reliability, rather than the validity of the estimates.

Comparisons of RWTP with actual payments is a useful exercise where the RWTP values are intended for use in a cost-benefit analysis. However, if CVM is being used, as it is here, as a surrogate referendum mechanism for use in public participation exercises then the appropriate comparison is against existing techniques and procedures used for this purpose. The fact that RWTP does seem to approximate to TWTP could be considered to be important if, as part of the outcome of using a monetary-based cardinal scale, the actual level of spending, as well as intensity of feeling, is sought.

3.7.2 Researcher-based Sources of Error

This subsection details the sources of error that are dependent on the design, execution and context of the CVM interview. Again, any particular categorisation is arbitrary due to the many interrelated issues but the amount of literature relating to informational problems in applications of the CVM justifies separate mention here. The other area deserving comment concerns starting point or anchoring bias. The embedding problem, a major cause of concern for those using the CVM, was dealt with in Section 3.1 as this issue relates to the measurement of subcomponents of either total economic value or of a policy.

3.7.2.1 Information-Related Error

The degree of information provided to a respondent in a CVM survey, along with the way that information is provided and received, will affect the RWTP. This sort of statement is consistent with the line of argument provided in the earlier discussion on the hypothetical nature of the CVM. As Hanley and Munro (1991) argue, where respondents find scenarios too hypothetical to take seriously, the importance of information becomes paramount. Furthermore, where the scenario is plausible to a respondent but the utility to be derived from the outcome of some change is uncertain, information can affect the probabilities attached to various benefits. A further area showing the importance of information relates to strategic behaviour. Where a respondent may be considering underbidding, informing that respondent of the consequences (non-provision of the good perhaps) may lead to more truthful answers.

The conclusion from a study by Bergstrom *et al.* (1990) supports the case that information provision can affect RWTP. Given in the appendix to their paper are the two sets of 'service information' provided to respondents. Service information is defined by the authors as:

> ...[information which] describes consumption services or attributes which can be derived from a given environmental commodity with fixed, objectively measurable characteristics. (p 620)

The authors conclude:

> The results indicate that SI [service information] increased WTP for wetland protection.

In this study by Bergstrom *et al.*, only service information relating to beneficial consumption services was provided. This was also the case in the Hanley and Munro (1991) study which provided information on endangered butterflies but intentionally omitted similar information for snakes and spiders. Conclusions such as that drawn by Bergstrom *et al.* should not then be generalised to situations where both 'positive' and 'negative' information is provided.

The classification of information into these two categories of positive and negative information is a subjective procedure. What is positive for one respondent may be negative for another. The provision of information and, as importantly, how it is received by the respondent will determine if the answers given reflect that which is being sought by the researcher. Mitchell and Carson (1989) provide a useful schema to illustrate this point and this is outlined in Figure 3.12 in which correct information perceived as intended is the optimum outcome.

Belson (1968) for instance found that in the best-understood questions in a survey, only fifty percent of respondents interpreted the question as intended by the researcher. This perception problem is referred to as Mental Account Bias. The contents of Table 3.6 are adapted from Carson (1991) and Collins *et al.* (1992) and serve to illustrate the potential range of information-related sources of bias.

Scenario element

A. Information provided in the survey instrument: (1) Correct   (2) Incorrect (theoretical misspecification)

B. Perceived by respondent: (1) As intended   (2) Not as intended by the researcher (methodological misspecification)

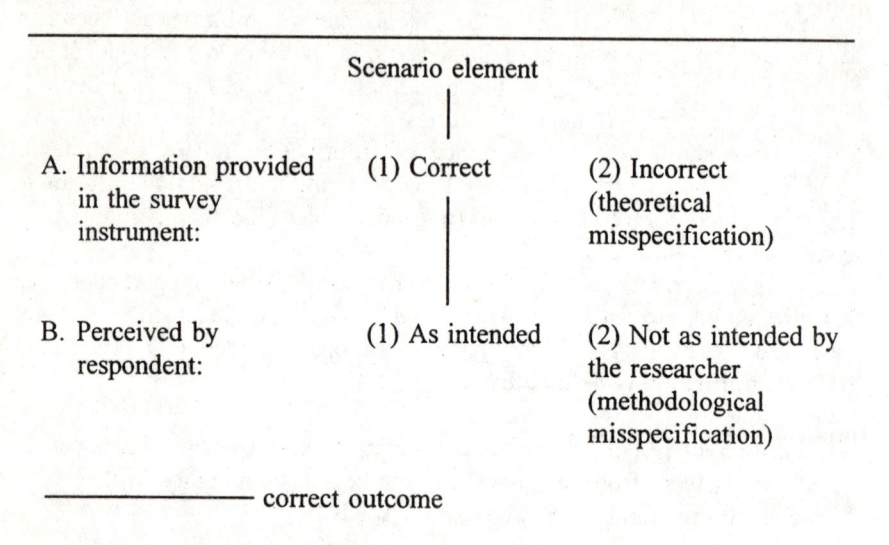

————————— correct outcome

Figure 3.12: The Relationship between Theoretical and Methodological Mis-specification
Source: Mitchell and Carson (1989) p 247

It is not sufficient to conclude, as Bergstrom *et al.* (1990) do that increasing the amount of service information would increase the RWTP. How that information is conveyed to the respondent, the information media, will also have an effect on RWTP. Where lengthy verbal descriptions are given to respondents the effect could be one of tedium, resulting in ill-thought out RWTP responses.

Collins *et al.* (1992) propose to overcome the need for verbal descriptions by using multi-media technology, essentially interactive computer software, in their study of values for urban aesthetics in Portsmouth. However, fear of such technology as computers, 'technophobia', may itself result in errors due to poor interactions (inability) or sampling error (non-response).

Vining and Orland (1989) have examined the use of video to aid visual impact assessment. They conclude that there is little difference in respondent-rated tests of the quality of video versus the more common, colour slide photography. They are also careful to note that visual presentation of an amenity is not sufficient where the majority of the total economic value is symbolic or non-visual. In one of the two CVM experiments reported in Chapter 5, an interactive computer package was used. In the other experiment, a 'hard' copy of the computer generated graphics was used. There was no observable difference in the ease which respondents displayed in using either of the two approaches.

If it is found that information provision (and, as importantly, respondent's comprehension) do increase the RWTP, this may form the basis of a call for general public education with regard to the environment. The case for moral suasion as a legitimate policy instrument (the increased use of bottle banks, for example, in the UK) could be seen as a reflection of increased values for the environment following awareness raising in the previous years.

Table 3.6
Potential Sources of Information Related Bias in CVM Surveys

Type of bias	Comment
Implied Value Cue Biases	
Relational	Where the description of the good presents information about its relationship to other public or private commodities that influences a respondent's WTP amount.
Importance	Where the act of being interviewed or some feature of the instrument suggests to the respondent that one or more levels of the amenity has value.
Position	Where the position or order in which valuation questions for different levels of good (or different goods) suggest to respondents how those levels should be valued.
Scenario Mis-specification Biases	
Symbolic	Where a respondent values a symbolic entity instead of the researcher's intended good.
Part-whole	Where a respondent values a larger or a smaller entity than the researcher's intended good.

Geographical Part-whole	Where a respondent values a good whose spatial attributes are larger or smaller than the spatial attributes of the researcher's intended good.
Benefit Part-whole	Where a respondent includes a broader or a narrower range of benefits in valuing a good than intended by the researcher.
Metric	Where a respondent values the amenity on a different and typically more imprecise scale than the one intended by the researcher.
Probability of Provision	Where a respondent values a good whose probability of provision differs from that intended by the researcher.
Context Misspecification	Where the perceived context of the market differs from the intended context.
Payment Vehicle	Where the payment vehicle is either misperceived or is itself valued in a way not intended by the researcher.
Property Right	Where the property right perceived for the good differs from that intended by the researcher.
Method of Provision	Where the intended method of provision is either misperceived or is itself valued in a way not intended by the researcher.
Budget Constraint	Where the perceived budget constraint differs from the budget constraint the researcher intended to invoke.
Elicitation Question	Where the perceived elicitation question fails to convey a request for a firm commitment to pay the highest amount the respondent will realistically pay before preferring to do without the amenity.
Instrument	Where the intended context or reference frame conveyed by the preliminary nonscenario material differs from that perceived by the respondent.

Source: Adapted from Carson (1991) and Collins et al. (1992)

3.7.2.2 Starting Point and Range Biases

Starting point and range biases, the 'anchoring' phenomena, are well documented in the psychometrics literature (Poulton (1977)) and in the CVM literature (Green and Tunstall (1991)).

Starting point and range biases are the outcome of attempts to facilitate the respondent's valuation process. According to Desvousges *et al.* (1983) open-ended questionnaire formats, where the respondent is just asked for a maximum amount she is willing to pay for the specified good, have resulted in a large number of protest bids. These are zero bids, or conversely, unrealistically high bids given a respondent's income. These bids increase the variance of the error term giving unreliable estimates.

In response to this problem, CVM researchers have proposed a number of alternative elicitation procedures. An iterative bidding procedure, where the interviewer uses a starting value and asks the respondent to indicate if she is willing to pay that amount, is susceptible to starting point bias. According to Green and Tunstall (1991) this is where the RWTP is correlated with the starting point value. Where starting point bias results in a shift of the mean bid, the distribution of bids should not necessarily be affected. Thus the result may be a reliable but invalid estimate of TWTP.

Payment card systems have also been proposed. Here the respondent is shown a card on which a range of payments is illustrated. Whilst the respondent is free to choose her own starting point, payment cards have been found to introduce a number of possible biases. These result from:

i) the lowest sum stated on the card;
ii) the highest sum stated on the card;
iii) the mid-point sum stated on the card; and
iv) the increment between sums stated on the card.

Kahneman (1986) concludes that payment cards are not a good substitute for open-ended questionnaire formats for these reasons.

Where a large sample is available, the 'take-it-or-leave-it' approach developed by Bishop and Heberlein (1979) may be used. Here, each respondent is randomly assigned a value around a previously established feasible range and mean for the good. A simple 'yes' or 'no' response is required to the question of whether or not that respondent is willing-to-pay the amount stated for the specified good. This is also the approach recommended by Arrow *et al.* (1993).

Kealy and Turner (1993) found that the responses given by the same individuals to the open-ended and then the dichotomous choice format were significantly different from each other. This was only true in the valuation of public goods. In private goods markets no difference was found. Kealy and Turner suggest that the findings with regard to public goods are due to a respondent's lack of familiarity with the open-ended question format and, further, that open-ended questions introduce an incentive for strategic behaviour. However, dichotomous choice formats are not without problems. Because the dependent variable is not continuous, the error term in an OLS model would determine the likely non-normal distribution. Ozuna *et al.* (1993) thus recommend that misspecification tests be applied to dichotomous choice models. Developments in the application of dichotomous choice formats have led Kanninen (1993) to advocate a double-bounded format where the second bid elicited is dependent upon the response to the first. Kanninen shows this method to be statistically more efficient than the single-bounded model. This approach has also seen recent development by Langford *et al.* (1994) who have extended the model to a triple-bounded format.

Given the many potential pitfalls in the use of the CVM, the following section provides a summary of the key issues which must be addressed by practitioners.

3.8 A Guide to Good Practice

This section provides an overview of issues to be considered in the application of CVM surveys. Table 3.7 draw heavily on the work of Green and Tunstall (1991). The extension to their work lies in the review of market research ethics and the market research code of conduct. This last focus is felt to be an important omission in the CVM literature. As the CVM involves contact with the public in a survey, interviewer-interviewee, situation, the similarity with market research, and thus its associated conduct and problems, is obvious.

The issues raised in Table 3.7 refer to the design of the survey instrument from the point of view of the researcher. No mention is made by Green and Tunstall (nor, apparently, in any other CVM-related literature) concerning the right of the interviewee.

Tybout and Zaltman (1974) have compared the issues addressed by both the American Marketing Association (AMA) and the Market Research Society (European), (MRS). Table 3.8 summarises their findings concerning the rights of the respondent.

According to Tybout and Zaltman, violation of any of these rights may lead to a number of problems. For example, where there is a perceived invasion of privacy, in-depth questioning on a respondent's value system in a CVM study perhaps, then the likely outcome is a stressful interview situation with potentially invalid or unreliable results and a refusal to participate in future research.

Table 3.7
Methodological Requirements for CVM Surveys of Recreation Value

Design of survey instrument

- Knowledge of the public's definition (perception) of the good to be valued required -if not known, an exploratory survey is required to determine what is the good

- Knowledge of the public's preference for the good is required - if not known, an exploratory survey is required

- Include checks on whether preference for the activity associated with the good actually depends on the availability of the good

- Include internal checks of the validity of the instrument: criterion and construct validity

- Design instrument on basis of underlying model of hypothesized determinants of preferences for the good and constraints and include behavioural correlates of preferences

- Include questions on respondent's present and past experience and use of the good

- Include at least interval level measures of current enjoyment and either of enjoyment after the change or of the proportional change in enjoyment expected

- Specify expected functional form of relationships

- Use payment vehicle which corresponds to how goods would actually be paid for

- Include check of attitudes towards payment vehicle

- Include an appropriate measure of income

- If appropriate definition of the problem is a willingness to accept compensation and not willingness to pay, then accept that the study will be experimental

- Include clear definition of the change in the good being considered (eg use of drawings/photographs)

- Tell respondents what is the current situation including how much they are contributing at present (economic theory specifies that the public should have perfect information)

- Legitimate a refusal to pay

- Use a filter question as whether the respondent is willing to pay before asking how much

- Randomly assign one of the several variants of the willingness to pay question

- Either use a willingness to pay question which has worked before or do an exploratory study to validate new version against known version

- Ask respondents the reasons why they were willing to pay and how much they were willing to pay

- Take note of rules on gross length, wording and question order in designing instrument

- If want to determine nonuse values, then determine an overall willingness to pay for the good. Do not seek to derive separate estimates of use and nonuse values

- Do a pretest

Sampling

- Define the population who may benefit

- Define appropriate subgroups within that population

- Use large samples because of high variance expected in willingness to pay

- Determine representative sample of target population(s) or times/places/days at which surveys are to be undertaken

Fieldwork

- Use interview surveys (or validate the results of a postal or telephone survey against identical interview survey)

- Use experienced fieldworkers

- Check quality of previous fieldwork

- Give them clear instructions

- Brief them on survey and instrument design

- ID cards, letters to police, respondents all required

- Check returns for errors in interviews

- Make call-back checks to see that those who were said to have been interviewed were interviewed

Analysis

- Check for punching errors

- Start with Exploratory Data Analysis

- Use statistical techniques appropriate to data

- If using parametric statistical analysis, transform data to normality

- Check sample is representative of population

- Base analysis on underlying model: define both additive and interactive relationships - make sure statistical model is the same as the theoretical model

- Check whether results from any analysis both conform to underlying theory and statistically fit adequately (eg look at residuals) - R^2 is not enough

- Occam's Razor applies to the inclusion of variables

- If explanations are poor fit, throw away the results

- Check that internal validity checks are satisfactory; if not, throw away the results

- Compare values from this survey with values from same instrument used to value different good - if values same, then instrument invalid

- Compare results from different willingness to pay questions for agreement - should be the same

Source: Green and Tunstall (1991)

Although Green and Tunstall do refer to the need to use "experienced fieldworkers" (see Table 3.7) it may be in the long term interests of UK CVM researchers to ensure that only MRS cardholding interviewers are used.

Table 3.8
AMA and MRS Focus on Subject's Rights in Market Research

	Addressed by:	
1. **The Right to Choose to Participate**	**AMA**	**MRS**
(i) Awareness of right	NO	YES
(ii) Sufficient information provided to enable choice	NO	YES
(iii) Opportunity given to choose to participate	NO	YES
2. **The Right to Safety**		
(i) Protection of anonymity	YES	YES
(ii) Freedom from stress	NO	YES
(iii) Freedom from deception	NO	YES
3. **The Right to be informed**		
(i) Debriefing	NO	NO
(ii) Dissemination of Data	YES	NO

Source: Tybout and Zaltman (1974)

3.9 Summary and Conclusions

In order to assess how useful the CVM would be in enhancing public participation in local planning, it is necessary to examine the characteristics of the method in relation to the requirements discussed briefly in Section 3.0 and at more length in Chapter 1.

A combination of these requirements suggests that any method of preference revelation should be capable of eliciting intensity of preference directly from members of the public. These preferences should be recorded on a cardinal scale and, for a number of reasons such as respondents' familiarity with money and the additional benefits that knowledge of the absolute size of overall expenditure can bring, the scale should be money-based. The CVM fulfils these requirements. Surveys are conducted directly with a sample of the relevant population and their responses are money bids, normally a maximum willingness to pay, for some proposal. Thus the CVM also meets a further requirement that respondents should feel an 'active' part of the decision-making process. Given that the responses are recorded as money figures, it is also relatively easy to conduct, and present the results of, sensitivity analyses for decision makers.

A final requirement was that any method chosen to reveal preferences should provide for safeguards against strategic behaviour by respondents. Whilst it can never be guaranteed that all respondents answer honestly, the discussion in Section 3.7.1.1 considered the likelihood of respondents behaving strategically in a CVM survey. Given that best practice (summarized in Section 3.8) is adopted, there appears to be little scope or incentive for respondents to behave strategically in a CVM survey.

Although in the review of Arrow's impossibility theorem in Chapter 1, the issue of cost of preference revelation was not covered, it would undoubtedly be a deterrent for financially constrained planning authorities if they were to consider adopting the CVM as part of their public participation exercises. As such, in Section 3.6 the practice of benefit transfer (BT) was considered as a possible alternative to original studies being undertaken in all instances. In these early days of BT, its use is deemed to be most appropriate in cases where similar changes were being proposed at 'policy' sites to those which had been valued at similar 'study' sites.

The CVM, used in conjunction with BT, may be a useful and low-cost approach to preference elicitation. However, the CVM is not without conceptual problems and practical pitfalls. The skill in the design of the survey will determine the validity and the reliability of the results. There are, of course, trade-offs to be made in terms of the required level of accuracy of the estimates and the amount of resources to be dedicated to the survey. This trade-off will also determine, to some extent, the size of the sample chosen and, therefore, the number of people who will have taken an active part in the decision-making process. At the extreme, where very few resources are available or where decision makers prefer to use BT, the level of active involvement is significantly reduced.

On a different note, the CVM as currently practiced, may lead to its own demise. The CVM is a relatively new technique and relatively few members of the general public have ever taken part in this type of survey. As this number grows, the hypothetical nature of payment for a stated public good may cause severe difficulties. Unless the CVM results influence public policy and respondents actually contribute, perhaps via higher taxes, to environmental improvements, belief in the method will decline. At such a time, the incentives for strategic behaviour, especially for minimizing effort (ME in Table 3.5) will increase.

4 Factorial Survey Design

4.0 Introduction

This chapter provides an overview of the second of the two research methods employed in this work, factorial surveys. It is not the intention here to develop the factorial survey approach. Instead, the objective is to summarise the theoretical underpinning of the technique and to suggest how it can be used in conjunction with the contingent valuation method in the context of this research.

Firstly then, a brief rationale is given for choosing to use factorial surveys given that an objective of this research is to provide a practical tool for planners for use in the public participation process. Section 4.2 provides a review of the underlying theory and, in the final section, it is shown how the two methods, factorial surveys and contingent valuation, can be used together to elicit values for subcomponents (attributes) of a good. In the context of this work, the relevant good is a number of alternative local plans. This final section draws on the debate between Goodman (1989, 1992) and Freeman (1991).

For its likely acceptance by planners, the addition to the public participation process proposed here must be cost-effective. The transfer of benefit estimates between plans is thus seen as desirable, if not essential. Section 3.6 dealt with the issue of benefit transfer in detail, but the relevance of mentioning this technique again here is because its success in this planning context is largely dependent upon an attribute approach to valuation. Not only does factorial survey design lend itself to this attribute approach, it also facilitates an inexpensive, experimental, laboratory-based valuation exercise. The results of such an experiment are reported in Chapter 5.

4.1 Modelling Individual Choice

Stewart's (1983) model of individual choice, Figure 4.1, focuses on the evaluation of subjective attributes of alternative goods. In his model, which is conceptually similar to that of Lancaster (1966), vectors of subjective attributes (and presumably, levels of each attribute) are evaluated by an individual as a necessary pre-requisite to choice. Use of this model would suggest that all alternatives of, say, structure or local plans, (A_1, A_2,...., A_n), could be ranked, revealing the individual's preference schedule. However, whilst it is necessary to know the final, ordinal, ranking of preferences (evaluation of vectors) in order to make a choice, it would be more useful to record preferences on a cardinal scale and to know the contribution to final ranked position of the component attributes of each vector.

	Alternatives	Subjective Attributes	Evaluation Function	Integration	Choice
	A_1	y_1	$f_1(y_1)$		A_1
Problem Formulation	A_2	y_2	$f_2(y_2)$	$G(f_1, f_2, ..., f_m)$	A_2
	A_3	y_3	$f_3(y_3)$		A_3
	.	y_4	.		.
	.	.	.		.
	A_n	.	.		A_n
		y_m	$f_m(y_m)$		

Figure 4.1: A Model of Individual Choice
Source: Stewart (1983)

It is important to know these attribute values in order that preferences elicited in one study be transferable to situations where the attributes, (and levels of attributes), of alternatives, vary from the original situation. One method of achieving such a valuation bank is to estimate the contribution to overall value resulting from changes in levels of each attribute.

Hanley and Ruffell (1993) adopted a similar approach to the valuation of selected forests in the UK. In the first of their two experiments, they showed respondents in a CVM survey, photographs depicting varying levels of forest characteristics. In their second experiment, characteristics levels were used as predictors of WTP. Although they conclude that characteristics levels are poor predictors of WTP, this result may have been due to the nature of the good where, perhaps, respondents were unable to discern changes in forest type or density, rather than a problem with the method employed.

Another model of preference elicitation, and a more relevant example given the context of this research, is given by Lichfield (1992) where 'effects' rather than 'attributes' are evaluated (see Figure 4.2). The outcome is the same however, with a choice being made between alternatives, (plans).

PROPOSALS:	DEVELOPMENT OPTION A	ALTERNATIVE OPTION B
EFFECTS ON:	Transport, Industry, Housing The Environment, etc.	Transport, Industry, Housing The Environment, etc.
COMMUNITY EXPERIENCE:	SAMPLES FROM THE RELEVANT COMMUNITY By: Age, Sex, Income, Interests, Ethnicity, Employment Status....etc.	
PREFERENCES:	A A B B B B A A B B	

Figure 4.2: Lichfield's Community Impact-Analysis Procedure
Source: Adapted from Lichfield (1992)

In Lichfield's model, effects are analogous to the evaluation of changes in levels of attributes in Stewart's model. However, a criticism of both models is that the outcome of each process is stated solely in terms of all or nothing preference for one of the alternatives. No indication of intensity of preference is sought.

Given that Stewart's model does accurately represent the choice process of an individual, and given that certain socio-economic conditions determine, to some extent, the evaluation of vectors by an individual, it is possible, according to Rossi and Nock (1982), to evaluate incremental changes in the level of single attributes. The design method advocated by Rossi and Nock is the factorial survey approach. Methods of analysis on the data collected can vary but the simplest, and that provided as an example in chapter 5, is OLS multiple regression analysis.

4.2 Factorial Surveys: Design and Analysis

In the relevant application of factorial surveys for the purpose of this research, individuals would be presented with a number of hypothetical goods (perhaps structure or local plans) consisting of a number of attributes (for instance, areas of green space, industrial land, housing, out-of-town-retail). Each representation of a plan would consist of a randomly selected level of each attribute and individuals drawn from a sample would each be asked to value a number of these hypothetical plans.

Underpinning the factorial survey method is the belief that human judgments are structured. Furthermore, choice between alternatives is considered to be based on the evaluation of a small number of the associated attributes. Proponents of the method also assume that many judgments are to some extent socially determined. As Rossi and Nock (1982) state:

> .....there is more or less agreement among persons on how much weight should be given to relevant characteristics and on how such characteristics should be combined in order to make judgments. (p 17)

The social determinants of judgment are therefore reflected in the coefficients (weights) attached to each attribute in the analysis and in the functional form of the model. A third assumption concerning judgments is that individuals do vary from the socially determined norm but do so in a regular way. As Goodman (1989) states:

> .....individuals may depart from the societal norms, but do so, among alternatives, in a logical and consistent manner. (p 61)

In a well specified model, a high explained variance (high R^2 value) could be interpreted as strong consensus among individuals with regard to the weightings attached to each attribute. ($(1-R^2)$ would represent the deviations from consensus and random error.)

In its simplest form, the value of a good, in this context a local plan, comprising of K attributes, would be shown for an individual, i, as V_i in:

$$V_i = b_0 + b_1X_1 + ... + b_KX_K + e_i \qquad (4.1)$$

given that the valuation function is additive. Additive separability is a strong restriction on the form of preferences although it cannot be ruled out on *a priori* grounds. It is necessary in factorial surveys to ensure little or no correlation between the explanatory variables. This poses some problems where the model is more correctly specified as a multiplicative one or where pairs of attributes form an interactive explanatory variable. In Stewart's model, the integration function for the latter case would become:

$$G(f_1, f_2, ..., f_1f_2, ..., f_n, ..., f_nf_{n-x})$$

Ensuring little correlation among explanatory variables is achieved using factorial surveys by generating a large sample of, say, plans each consisting of randomly generated attribute levels. If, for instance, there are x levels used to describe an attribute then the probability of any level being generated should be 1/x and the distribution of levels of an attribute throughout the analysis would tend towards being rectangular. Therefore, according to Rossi and Nock, the correlations among attributes would asymptotically approach zero as the sample size increases.

In the context of this research, it is important to add a number of socio-economic factors into Equation (4.1). This addition (Equation 4.2) will highlight the contribution (positive or negative) to the total economic value given for any plan which is due to the socio-economic characteristics of an individual in the sample. This should facilitate the transferability of the results to areas with a different mix of socio-economic characteristics. As the socio-economic variables are not correlated with the attributes, orthogonality is not compromised. Instead, this addition should result in relatively unchanged coefficients on the attributes and an increase in the R^2 value. Equation (4.1) is thus expanded to become:

$$V_{ik} = \alpha + \Sigma \beta_k x_k + \gamma C_i + \delta S + \epsilon_{ik} \qquad (4.2)$$

$$(i = 1, 2, ..., I; k = 1, 2, ..., K)$$

where V_{ik} is the valuation of plan k by individual i;
x_k represents the randomly generated attributes of plan k;
C_i denotes the socio-economic characteristics of individual i;
S is a binary variable taking the value one where a respondent is aware of equivalent substitute facilities, and a value of zero otherwise;
α, β, γ, and δ are parameters, whilst ϵ_{ik} is a random error term.

4.3 Linking Factorial Survey Design and the Contingent Valuation Method

Goodman (1989) demonstrated the use of factorial survey design in conjunction with hedonic pricing in a bid to estimate the components of housing attribute bundles. In his research, individuals were asked to rate, (using a scale of 1-9), randomly selected bundles of attributes. Each bundle, (or vignette or vector), represents a hypothetical house. A sample of N individuals each providing M ratings gave NM observations which were then analysed using the equation:

$$R_{ijt} = g(Z,C) \tag{4.3}$$

where R is the rating for individual i, in location j at time t. Z is the vector of attributes (X_k in Equation 4.2) and C represents the vector of socio-economic characteristics (C_i in Equation 4.2).

Goodman argues that by linking this set of ratings to actual data for the characteristics and selling price of houses with similar attributes it would allow for the valuation of marginal changes in the level of any of the attributes. For instance, he illustrates the marginal willingness to pay (Wz_{j-50}) for the last 50 square feet of space as the ratio of the two marginal ratings (R), (one taken at z_j and the other at z_{j-50}) multiplied by the hedonic price (P) evaluated at the reference level z_j. The actual formula given by Goodman is:

$$Wz_{j-50} = (\partial R/\partial z_{j-50})/(\partial R/\partial z_j) \cdot Pz_j \tag{4.4}$$

However, in a comment on Goodman's paper, Freeman (1991) suggests that the marginal willingness to pay estimated by Goodman was incorrect due to the fact that individuals were asked to trade off attributes in the initial rating exercise without any reference to a money numeraire. Freeman states:

> Thus the individual does not reveal anything about relative monetary values of housing characteristics by his choice of an integer rating for a housing bundle. The ratings bear no logical relationship to the income-constrained utility maximising choices that are the foundation of standard welfare measurement theory. (p 25)

Surprisingly, Freeman does not even mention the existing criticisms of the hedonic price approach. These were examined in Chapter 3 and are not dealt with in detail here. It is sufficient merely to raise the issues of subjectivity in classifying some of the data in hedonic price studies, (for instance specifying neighbourhood characteristics), and the interaction between housing and, especially, labour markets.

On a positive note, Freeman, by suggesting that a money numeraire (for example a good of known monetary value) be included in the vector of attributes to be rated is, in effect, advocating a process similar to contingent ranking, (Rae 1983). Here, where the same ranking is given to two vectors of attributes but where some of the numeraire has been traded-off for a marginal change in one of the attributes, the value of that change in the attribute is simply the monetary equivalent as measured in terms of the numeraire.

In a later paper by Goodman (1992) the necessary inclusion of a money numeraire is taken up. However, instead of pursuing Freeman's suggestion of contingent ranking, Goodman advocates the use of contingent valuation questions. Contingent values, he suggests, should be elicited for vectors of attributes which depart from an observable reference level. The value elicitation part of his questionnaire takes the following format:

> Suppose, suddenly, your home was no longer available, but it was costless to move. Given your current income, how much rent would you be willing to pay for a unit with the following characteristics [vector Z_j]? (p 96)

Setting the change in utility to zero ($\partial U = 0$), thus estimating the true Hicksian compensated demand curve, is achieved by the condition that it is 'costless to move'. Goodman then goes on to give an equation for this demand curve derived from variations between willingness to pay for some vector (Z_j) and the reference level (Z_j^*).

Goodman, however, advocates that the value for the reference level be determined using hedonic pricing. Given the theoretical properties discussed in Chapter 3 with regard to the CVM, there would appear to be little justification for adhering to hedonic price determined reference levels. Contingent valuations may to some extent be affected by sources of error such as starting-point bias, but given the problems involved in estimating hedonic price functions, this does not constitute grounds for substituting hedonic price estimates for those which would be achieved using the CVM. Indeed, if it is accepted that the CVM can approximate true willingness-to-pay values, the factorial survey and the CVM methods used together offer significant opportunities for estimating the marginal valuation of levels of attributes of non-market goods.

5 Enhancing Public Participation

5.0 Introduction

This chapter begins with a brief description of the geographical area chosen for this research exercise. The public participation which took place in the development process of the local plan for that area is also examined. In Section 5.2 the objectives of the research and the methods to be employed to achieve those objectives are reiterated. The bulk of the chapter then focuses on the design constraints and on the analysis of results.

5.1 The Bristol North Fringe Local Plan

The Bristol North Fringe Local Plan (1987) describes North Avon District Council's proposals for the development and other use of land in the area during the period up to the mid-1990's.

In the development of this Plan the Council fulfilled its statutory duty with respect to public participation. In the Plan it is stated that:

> The Council has a duty to ensure that adequate publicity is given to the matters [it] proposes to include in the Local Plan. [It] must also ensure that local residents, organisations and other interested bodies are given an adequate opportunity to comment on these proposals and thereby influence the content of the Plan (para 1.11 p 2)

There were three stages involved in meeting this obligation. First, in January 1983, a leaflet drop to households invited initial comments. This was followed in May 1985 with a further invitation to comment on specific proposals contained in an initial document, the *Report for Consultation*. The third stage consisted of a Public Local Inquiry which took place in June and July 1986.

The idea that this three-stage process is adequate for capturing the public's preferences for development of a local environment was strongly challenged on both theoretical and empirical grounds in Chapters 1 and 2, where evidence was presented pointing to the inadequacies of existing public participation exercises. Many individuals and groups are excluded from the process. Where the public do manage to submit comments, these are received in haphazard form (face-to-face, written on official forms, written letters, telephone). The degree of importance given to public responses varies among planning bodies and appears to be based on subjective criteria. No satisfactory mechanism for weighting preferences is evident. Given the conclusions drawn by Arrow (1951) as discussed in Chapter 1, it is not surprising to find current methods of eliciting public preferences falling short of what is desirable.

Given this challenge to the existing public participation process, this research has focused on developing a suitable procedure for supplementing existing practice. A worked example of the proposed procedure is reported here.

5.2 Objectives of the Empirical Work

There are two objectives. The first is to illustrate an effective framework for increasing the general public's input into the development of local plans. The second is to consider the likely accuracy of a generalizable technique based on measures of preferences transferable between localities and, therefore, between plans. Success with regard to the first objective is determined by an examination of the use of the contingent valuation method (CVM) in this planning context, whilst consideration of the second objective relies on an analysis of the comparative results of two surveys using different samples from a similar population.[7]

The empirical work thus draws upon two methods discussed in previous chapters; the CVM and Factorial Survey Design (FSD). The former allows respondents' preferences to be elicited and monetized for non-market public goods. The latter is an experimental design method which produces randomly generated levels of attributes which make up a public good.

The public good in question here is a local plan. The main attribute of

---

[7] The words 'similar population' are used because the surveys were conducted in different years (1993 and 1995) and the extent of household turnover is unknown.

interest is the remaining undeveloped or 'green' space available within the area bounded by the plan. By effectively holding all but one of the other characteristics of the plan constant (amount of out-of-town retail space, amount of housing, amount of light industrial/business space), it is possible to map out, in monetary terms, the trade-off respondents are willing to pay (accept) for increases (decreases) in green space at the expense of the other variable. These trade-offs would then be represented in a number of valuation curves similar to that shown in Figure 3.5, Chapter 3. Given that the second survey is a repeat of the first in terms of the area chosen and the characteristics that are varied, evidence of the potential for benefit transfer (BT) would be supported by the valuation curves from each survey proving to be similar.

5.3   Design of the Application

As previously stated, the design of the application used here to elicit valuations for changes in attribute levels of a plan is based upon the use of the CVM and FSD. In addressing the major issues raised in the reviews of these two methods, the design, given the objectives of practicality and transferability, has been subject to tight constraints.

It was hoped, in the initial stages of this work, that it would be possible for respondents to be asked to value changes in the levels of attributes for district-wide plans or even the larger-scale structural plans. However, it soon became apparent that such an exercise would not satisfy the necessary theoretical conditions for a valid CVM survey, primarily because of the then necessarily blurred geographical representations. The FSD is less imposing on the design of the application. As long as the relevant attributes can be identified and measured in some objective way for any plan, then the only constraint imposed by the FSD is that changes in each attribute should be randomly presented to respondents. Given that both surveys were designed to change only one variable at a time, use of FSD posed few problems. Meeting the requirements of the CVM posed some serious difficulties, however. These difficulties and their solutions are detailed below.

It was suggested in Table 3.6, Chapter 3, that interviewers might be a source of bias in CVM surveys. In order to design out this potential bias, respondents in the first survey used an interactive computer application. However, whilst the effects of interviewer bias may be overcome to some extent, it is possible that other bias may have been imposed - such as that caused by fear of technology and thus self-selection in the sample.

In the first survey, the computer application contained background information on the area, descriptive text and graphical representations of each change in the level of attributes, and it provided for respondents' input and data storage. Use of this package also met the requirements for using FSD by allowing plans (maps) to be presented to respondents based on random levels of the relevant attributes. At the beginning of each respondent's session, maps of a wider area of Bristol and Northavon were illustrated in order to facilitate orientation. A questionnaire then followed which focused on the principal elements of any CVM survey, namely: construct validity (internal validity), attitudes towards the good in question, attitudes towards the proposed payment mechanism, frequency of use and reason for using the good, and household's income. Respondents were then presented with a randomly generated map, from a bank of sixty maps, and were asked to consider this map in relation to a reference map. Each respondent was asked to do this fifteen times.

In the second survey, the respondents were interviewed face-to-face.[8] Randomly generated maps from the same bank of sixty maps were used and the information pages and order of the questionnaire were identical to those adopted in the first survey. Apart from the second survey's using face-to-face interviewing, the only other factor which changed was the location of the survey. The first was conducted at the University of the West of England, Bristol, whilst the second survey took place in the coffee shop of Sainsburys plc. in the Bristol North Fringe area.

The bank of sixty maps was made up of three sets of twenty based upon the attributes: housing, light industrial/business park, out-of-town retail. Each set was further broken down by a 'block' or 'scattered' approach as discussed later. Each map depicted changes in green space based on 10% increments. Thus, any map presented to a respondent showed a combination of green space and one of the three other attributes, the latter either encroaching upon or receding from the green space in 10% increments either in a 'block' or in a 'scattered' approach. Increments of 10% were used as, in a pilot survey, smaller changes were found to be indiscernible, given the scale of the maps. (Information pages and the questionnaire are given in appendix 2.)

In both surveys, respondents were given the opportunity to return to the orientation pages or to previous maps to check on, and change if required, the values given. A benefit of the computer-based application rests with the respondent's choice to access information relating to each map in his or her own time without feeling pressured by the interviewer. In this way, the potential for information overload was avoided with this cut-off point being determined by the respondent rather than by the researcher or interviewer.

---

[8] It is acknowledged that, by changing the mode of interaction between interviewer and interviewee in the two surveys, this is likely to complicate any comparisons. However, this was necessary for practical reasons and, apart from this departure, the two processes were kept as similar as possible.

Similarly, respondents in the second survey were presented with the information pages and each was allowed to execute the survey at his or her preferred pace. This part of the design was based on the conclusions drawn by Whittington *et al.* (1992). In their study, two groups were given the same survey instrument. The first was a control group where immediate responses were sought. The second group of respondents was given a day to discuss the hypothetical changes posed to them before being asked to bid. Those in the second group gave significantly lower WTP bids. It is not suggested here that allowing time for refection before bidding would invariably reduce WTP. Indeed, it is easy to envisage instances where the converse might be true, for instance where the information presented to respondents is complex but, after assimilation, produces a positive influence on the bid. What is recognized, however, is that time for contemplation of the implications of any significant change is required in order to increase the reliability of the WTP bids.

The ability for respondents to determine the level of information they receive incorporates one of the recommendations made by the NOAA panel (Arrow *et al.* (1993)) on the use of the CVM. Furthermore, this ability for respondents to reflect upon valuations given and to change these if necessary builds in, to some extent, the feedback loop required by the Fishbein-Ajzen (1975) model discussed in Section 3.5.1.1. This feedback loop is a mechanism for incorporating the learning experience gained during the exercise by respondents and successfully addresses the 'familiarity' hypothesis proposed by Fishbein and Ajzen.

The two other hypotheses suggested by Fishbein and Ajzen, those of 'correspondence' and 'proximity', were addressed in the wording of the questionnaire. Correspondence refers to the likely correlation between the question asked and the intended inference to be drawn from the answer. Thus, in this questionnaire, respondents were given ample orientation about the overall area in question and were asked to value a specific change to a specific part of it.

Proximity was addressed via the payment question. 'Specified behaviour' is the label given by Fishbein and Ajzen to the nearest stage in an individual's decision process to actual payment. The payment question was made as realistic as possible, thus ensuring that respondents felt that they would have to make some payment, or receive compensation, dependent upon the final outcome.

Realism in the scenario, a belief by respondents that they may, in fact, have to pay the amount given as their valuation and, furthermore, that provision of the good in question is dependent upon the value they give, addresses the issue of potential strategic behaviour. (See Section 3.7.1.1.) After initial piloting of the questionnaire, the payment mechanism chosen was an annually determined payment to, or compensation from, a trust with charitable status. The trust would act as a management company for protection and maintenance of the available green space depicted in each map. Although Bateman *et al.* (1993), in their extensive survey of the Norfolk Broads in the UK, found a tax to be the most applicable payment mechanism, their study was focused on a national asset for which a national tax might be perceived to be the most appropriate method of payment. In this local planning context, respondents in the pilot study rejected such a tax as inappropriate and instead chose to buy the land via a trust. An annual, rather than lump-sum, payment was chosen for two reasons. First, using annual rather than lump-sum payments reduces the effort for respondents in discounting future benefits back to present values. Secondly, respondents do not have to build in a probability of moving out of the area. If they were to leave the area, they knew their payments, or compensation, would cease.

A further recommendation made by Arrow *et al.* (1993) is that dichotomous choice formats should be adopted in the valuation procedure (Bishop and Heberlein (1979)).[9] This approach requires a large sample size and the associated expense could not be justified at this experimental stage. Instead, respondents were given an open-ended format where they were asked either for their maximum willingness to pay for preferred changes in the amount of green space or their minimum willingness to accept for changes which they did not prefer in relation to the relevant reference map. It is recognized that such a design could lead to problems with reliability, which would be reflected in a large standard deviation in the results.

Another demanding constraint on the design of this application has been the need to project future land-use patterns in order to provide respondents with a reference point to which green space could be added or from which it could be taken away. Selecting completely hypothetical maps made up of various combinations of levels of attributes may be a useful approach for the design of a new town but it is unrealistic in a context where housing and other attributes already exist. For instance, asking respondents to value an increase in green space at the cost of removing a new housing estate is impractical. In practice, removing the housing estate is not a choice. Choice, in effect, only exists in areas where development plans are being debated and these, in most instances, consider removing green space and increasing the level of housing or some other attribute.

Respondents were thus presented with a hypothetical situation where half of the existing green space had been removed and replaced with one of the other attributes. From this reference point, which respondents were given

---

[9] An example of a dichotomous choice format is where a respondent is offered, say, £30 for a change in the quality of some environment. The respondent can accept or decline the offer. This is also referred to as the 'take it or leave it' or 'yes-no' format.

to believe was a credible position in ten years' time, respondents were asked to value both increases and decreases in the attribute, green space. They were thus expressing their willingness to pay to enjoy preferred changes from this reference point or their willingness to accept compensation otherwise.

In both surveys, and immediately before the payment question, respondents were reminded to consider substitutes for the green space they were valuing.

The second of the objectives of this work relates to the transferability of results between plans and thus between locations and between populations. This is deemed to be important as a cost-effective technique has a greater chance of being adopted by financially constrained planning authorities. As different locations may give rise to different socio-economic groups forming the sample population, a question relating to household income was also included. Given that the existing attributes, changes in these attributes, their associated valuations and socio-economic characteristics are all known, results from any one area should be transferable to another area. The discussion of benefit transfer (BT) in Section 3.6 concluded that, at least in the early stages of using BT in this context, most accuracy would be achieved with valuation transfers to areas with similar attributes, similar socio-economic characteristics and similar proposed changes.

More formally, the relationship between the value of green space and the determinants of that value can be expressed as in Equation (4.2) which is repeated here as Equation (5.1).

$$V_{ik} = \alpha + \Sigma \beta_k x_k + \gamma C_i + \delta S + \epsilon_{ik} \tag{5.1}$$

where V_{ik} is the valuation by individual i of map k; (i = 1, 2,...,I)
x_k represents the randomly generated attributes of map k;
(k = 1, 2,...,K)
C_i denotes the socio-economic characteristics of individual i;
S is a binary variable taking the value one where a respondent is aware of equivalent substitute facilities, and a value of zero otherwise;
α, β, γ, and δ are parameters, whilst ϵ_{ik} is a random error term.

In the literature relating to the transfer of benefits from original study sites to proposed policy sites, S would represent a vector of prices for substitutes.[10] However, equivalent substitutes in this instance are by definition zero priced, and, therefore, S represents solely the availability of

---

[10] For example, see Desvousges *et al.* (1992).

substitute facilities.

The error term, ϵ_{ik}, represents the impact of omitted explanatory variables, and both random measurement errors in V_{ik}, and any random influences on a respondent's valuation of each map. Where there are random errors in the respondent's valuations, there would be no bias in the regression coefficients. However, where measurement errors occur in the regressors, such bias would be introduced. Given that the socio-economic characteristics, C_i, were approximated here using income groups, as suggested by Walsh *et al.* (1992) in their review of benefit transfer studies, it is likely that some measurement error did exist. Only five income groups were used, resulting in a bunching of the data, which in turn left very little potential variation for this explanatory variable. This latter point is discussed in more detail below. Omitted variables would also cause bias in the regression coefficients in so far as these omitted variables were correlated with the included variables. In these surveys it seems likely that valuations would depend upon socio-economic characteristics other than income. This also will be discussed later.

Using the CVM, each of the *I* respondents in each survey was asked to value *K* changes in the vector of attributes **X**. Thus, *IK* observations relating to changes in **X** were generated in each case. The changes in **X** for any given observation were generated randomly and consisted of random combinations of green space and one other attribute.

On *a priori* grounds, two scenarios were examined where the physical attributes changed either in a simple 'block' approach or in a 'scattered' approach. The 'blocking' approach consisted of changes, in 10% increments, which appeared as one large block rather than being scattered throughout the green space. So, for instance, if the randomly generated change in attributes entailed giving up 40% of green space for housing, the housing was shown as a 40% block rather than as 40% scattered randomly throughout the area in question.

Therefore, given that respondents may have seen a map from any one of six different sets of maps for each of their valuations (three attributes changing in either a block or scattered manner), each set of maps in each survey had on average *IK*/6 observations. In the results reported below, *I* equals 24 and *K* equals 15 for each survey. Thus the average number of observations per set of maps in each survey was 60.

The socio-economic characteristics, C_i, were estimated for each respondent using household income as a proxy. Commercially available proxies such as that provided by ACORN (*A C*lassification *O*f *R*esidential *N*eighbourhoods) could also have been used, although the cost could not be justified at this experimental stage. ACORN data classify neighbourhoods by postcodes, providing a proxy for 'lifestyle' and, to some extent, income. In effect, ACORN data provide a picture of the range of housing in a given area and the number of households in each of the categories in the range. Of course, if actual household incomes are required in order to standardize monetized preferences, then a question eliciting such information may still be preferred.

In a study incorporating ACORN data, Collins and Evans (1993) used artificial neural network techniques to refute the conclusions of an earlier study by Pennington *et al.* (1990), who had suggested that aircraft noise around Manchester International Airport had no discernible impact on house prices. Collins and Evans' analysis shows that the ACORN groups associated with higher incomes (e.g. ACORN group 36: Detached houses - Exclusive suburbs) suffered one of the largest percentage (and therefore absolute) effects from aircraft noise. The fall in value for this class of property was approximately 12% at a Noise Number Index of 50. Where there is a high correlation between income and type of housing (ACORN group), it would not matter which is chosen to represent the socio-economic characteristics, C_i, in Equation (5.1). However, where it is important to gauge attitudes to changes in the physical environment, it is deemed more appropriate to use a proxy based on a composite index such as 'lifestyle' rather than to rely solely on income. This conclusion is substantiated in the results of the fieldwork detailed in Section 5.4 and the use of ACORN data is considered especially relevant given the planning context of this research.

It is worth noting one further point with regard to the use of income as a proxy for socio-economic characteristics. On *a priori* grounds, it would be expected that different responses would be obtained from different groups of respondents in CVM studies, given that varying preference patterns are evident for most goods. However, there is conflicting evidence with regard to the role of income as an explanatory variable. Bowker and MacDonald (1993), for instance, in their study of perceived health risks, found that income was insignificant as an explanatory variable of willingness to pay or to accept. Drake (1992), on the other hand, found income to be a significant determinant of willingness to pay for the preservation of the Swedish agricultural landscape.

Section 5.4 details the analysis of the data and interpretations of the results from each of the two surveys and includes a comparison of the two surveys in terms of the potential for BT.

5.4 Data Analysis and Interpretation of Results: Surveys 1 and 2

For the first survey, respondents were drawn from volunteers working at the University of the West of England, Bristol. Both academic and support staff were included. The fieldwork was conducted between 22 and 28 June 1993. The second survey was conducted with members of the public at Sainsbury's store in the Bristol North Fringe planning area on 26 and 27 September 1995.

Overall, some 360 observations were recorded for each survey, producing, on average, 60 observations for each of the six sets of maps in each survey. This output was generated on each occasion by asking each of 24 respondents to value 15 specified changes covering a random selection of maps depicting combinations of green space and one other attribute.[11]

An immediate problem is realized in that any conscious or unconscious bias for person i in valuation of a map k may be, to some extent, correlated with that same person's bias in valuing another map z.[12] That is, the condition for independence between observations, *viz*:

$$\text{Cov}(\epsilon_{ik}, \epsilon_{iz}) = 0 \quad \text{for all k, z (k} \neq \text{z)}$$

is unlikely to hold. Where such autocorrelation does exist, the use of *t* values may yield unreliable tests of significance. However, in order to achieve an equivalent number of observations without introducing this potential problem, a sample size of 360 people would have been required, which was considered impractical given the resources available for this work and given the objective of a 'gain in knowledge' rather than actual data for policy decisions, as discussed in Section 3.6 with regard to BT.

A potential consequence of autocorrelation, consistent over-valuation or under-valuation by a respondent would be inflated *t* values (Gujarati (1992)). However, any bias due to omitted variables could bias the *t* ratios in either direction. It is, therefore, unclear what the combined impact will be on the significance testing reported here.

An initial review of the data for survey 1 led to follow-up in-depth conversations with eight of the respondents. Six of these had invariably given zero valuations, one had shown major inconsistencies throughout, whilst another, in the lowest income group, had given extreme responses for all fifteen valuations.

---

[11] The use of a relatively small sample size, 24 respondents in each survey, was due to, primarily, resource constraints. No incentives were available to encourage respondents to take part in a relatively lengthy survey. Furthermore, for the first survey, the use of a specialized computer-based CVM instrument necessitated that the exercise be conducted at the University of the West of England, which determined the extent of the volunteer population. A final rationale relates to the need to explore a cost-effective approach which is satisfied, to some extent, by the use of multiple response from individual respondents.

[12] For example, an 'unconscious' bias might arise as a result of misinterpreting the hypothetical scenario, whereas a 'conscious' bias could arise through strategic behaviour.

The six giving zero valuations reported their unease with the valuation concept. All commented that it was not right to value nature in this way and, as such, they wanted no part in the survey. These six respondents' valuations were excluded from the statistical analysis. Whilst this elimination posed few problems here, the high proportion (25%) of those falling into this 'protest' group raises some concern for future research of this type. (Maxwell (1994) found a similar proportion of 'protest voters'.)

The respondent giving inconsistent answers, for instance giving WTP (positive) figures for some decrements and some increments in green space and likewise giving WTA (negative) figures for both decrements and increments, appeared to be unaware that this had been so. The respondent suggested, in follow-up, that perhaps he had not used the required negative sign for WTA consistently throughout the valuation exercise. This is seen as a problem with the prototype software. This respondent's observations were removed from the statistical analysis.

The final set of responses which gave cause for concern came from an individual in the lowest income group who consistently gave extreme valuations especially where compensation was sought. Further questioning revealed that she had recently been involved (only a few weeks prior to the survey) in a compulsory purchase controversy with regard to a small part of her garden. She agreed, in follow-up, that she had 'probably' overstated her preferences. This respondent's observations (both WTA and WTP) were also removed from the statistical analysis.

In Figure 5.1 the means for each of the six sets of maps from survey 1 are shown, along with an overall average encompassing the 240 observations deemed to be valid.

Four conclusions are immediately apparent. The first is that the use of a hypothetical reference level of 50% of green space under development in ten years' time has worked very well. Respondents were given the opportunity to say if they preferred a randomly chosen map to the relevant reference map. (The relevant reference map corresponded to the randomly chosen map in terms of the attribute replacing green space and also in terms of the block or scattered approach.) If they answered 'yes', they were given a question asking for maximum willingness to pay. If 'no', then a minimum willingness to accept was sought. Given that all valid observations fell in the north-east and south-west quadrants, as expected, this substantiates the hypothesis that the use of a hypothetical reference point can be interpreted properly by respondents.

Secondly, the use of an open-ended payment question has, as expected, led to a large variance in valuations. Although, from inspection of Figure 5.1, this appears to be most acute in the case of WTA, and whilst the absolute variation is far greater for WTA than it is for WTP, calculations of the coefficients of variation at various distances from the reference point do not

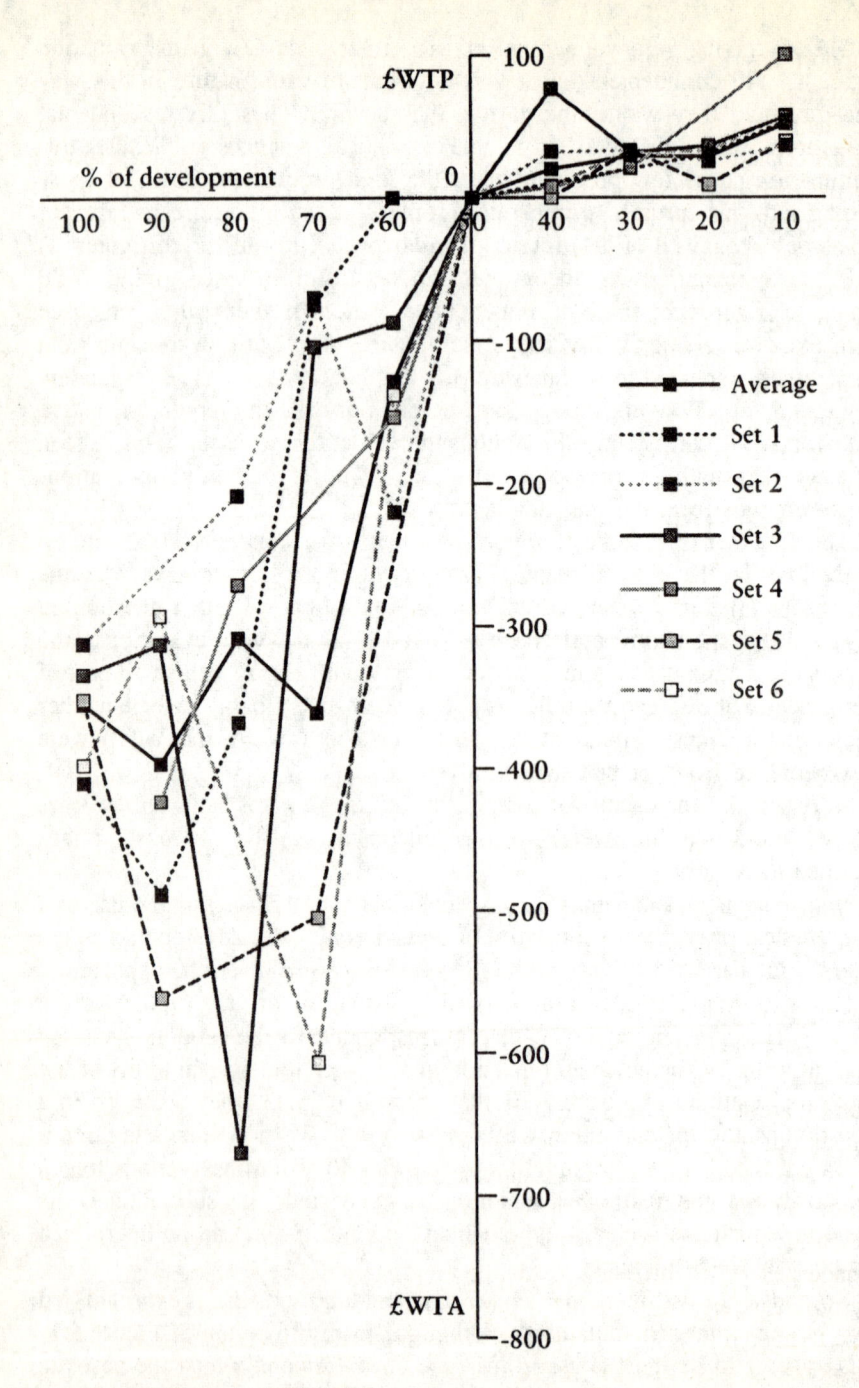

Figure 5.1: Survey 1 (N=240)

support any assertions about the relative reliability of either of the two measures.

The third conclusion is closely linked to the above discussion of WTP and WTA. The general shape of the average curve in Figure 5.1 is very similar to the theoretical valuation curve discussed in Chapter 3 (see Figure 3.5). For equivalent increments and decrements around some reference point, WTA is consistently greater than WTP. This outcome substantiates the theoretical arguments presented in Chapter 3 for the use of WTP rather than WTA even in cases where valuations for reductions in quantity or quality are being sought and where, instinctively, it is felt that property rights lie with respondents.

Lastly, it would seem that a respondent's valuations refer to green space and are not, in general, influenced by the attribute replacing that green space nor by whether this attribute is introduced in a block or as a scatter. This is evidenced for both surveys by the valuation curve for each set never being consistently above or below the respective average curve. This is important because it allows for the amalgamation of the data and for the subsequent statistical analysis to use all valid observations. Furthermore, it is important in cost-benefit analysis that the object being valued (in this case, green space) be valued in its own right and that the attribute replacing the green space be part of the 'cost' side of the equation rather than influencing the size of the benefits. For instance, a green-field site should be valued for the benefits it brings to those who enjoy it in any way. The value for that site should not be determined by what might replace it, a school or hospital, for instance, having a different effect than if a nuclear power station were contemplated. This is an important consideration, especially when research is conducted using the CVM, as the hypothetical change, if illustrated in too much detail, can easily influence responses. For example, Brookshire *et al.* (1976) professed to measure aesthetic values of a view, yet their research incorporated photographs of a proposed power station, so that their reported values are likely to include some element of liking for, or loathing of, power stations. Where it is the case that values incorporating the sight of a power station are required, then this should be shown, valued and reported as such but not as the value of the view alone.

Exactly the same criticism can be applied to the more recent work of Imber *et al.* (1991). In their study of the Kakadu Conservation Zone, respondents were given one of two scenarios to consider. Each was concerned with different levels of mining activity in the area. Thus, respondents were not giving a pure valuation of the conservation area but one tempered by their perceptions of mining activity. Indeed, some 15% of respondents gave as their reason for a positive WTP, the fact that they did not like mining or were against mining (Imber *et al.* (1991), table 5.7). These WTP bids are, then, WTP to stop mining not WTP to preserve the actual landscape in question.

In the second survey, four of the 24 respondents refused to offer valuations after initially accepting the invitation to take part. As with the six respondents who were labelled as 'protest voters' in the first survey, these four suggested it was wrong to apply valuations to nature. These respondents' zero valuations were removed from the statistical analysis. Only one other respondent gave cause for concern. Whilst offering apparently sensible and consistent WTP bids, this respondent refused to accept the concept of compensation on the grounds that the green space belonged to future generations as well as to the current generation. This is entirely consistent with one of the four reasons used to explain the divergence between WTP and WTA, which were considered in Section 3.4. Nine of the 15 valuations for this respondent were removed from the statistical analysis.

Figure 5.2 illustrates the means for each of the six sets of maps from survey 2. An overall average based on 291 valid observations is also shown.

The four conclusions drawn from inspection of Figure 5.1, for survey 1, also apply here. The hypothetical reference level appears to have worked well. The coefficients of variation for both WTA and WTP do not indicate that either is consistently more reliable. The average curve is of similar shape to that expected on *a priori* grounds as depicted in Figure 3.5. Finally, there is apparently no bias caused by the particular set of maps being valued.

Before considering the regression results, it may be helpful to examine Table 5.1 which shows some of the variables used in the regressions, along with their labels and frequencies. The frequencies are based on the number of respondents used in the statistical analyses.

For the first survey, nearly two-thirds of respondents lived within the Bristol North Fringe planning area. The remainder resided within a four mile radius. Sixtythree per cent stated that they had some use for the designated green space. The principal use was walking, with over half the respondents taking part in this activity. Two-thirds of respondents were unaware of equivalent substitute facilities. Interestingly, not all non-users indicated zero enjoyment from the area. An explanation is that these respondents held nonuse values for the area. All five income groups were represented, although the majority of respondents were evenly distributed across groups two, three and four. Eightyeight per cent found the proposed payment mechanism to be satisfactory.

Some differences are apparent for those taking part in the second survey. Ninetyfive per cent lived in the designated area and all respondents indicated that they used the green space. Similarities between the two samples include the fact that the predominant use of the green space was walking, that the majority of respondents were unaware of equivalent substitute facilities, and nearly all respondents were satisfied with the proposed payment mechanism.

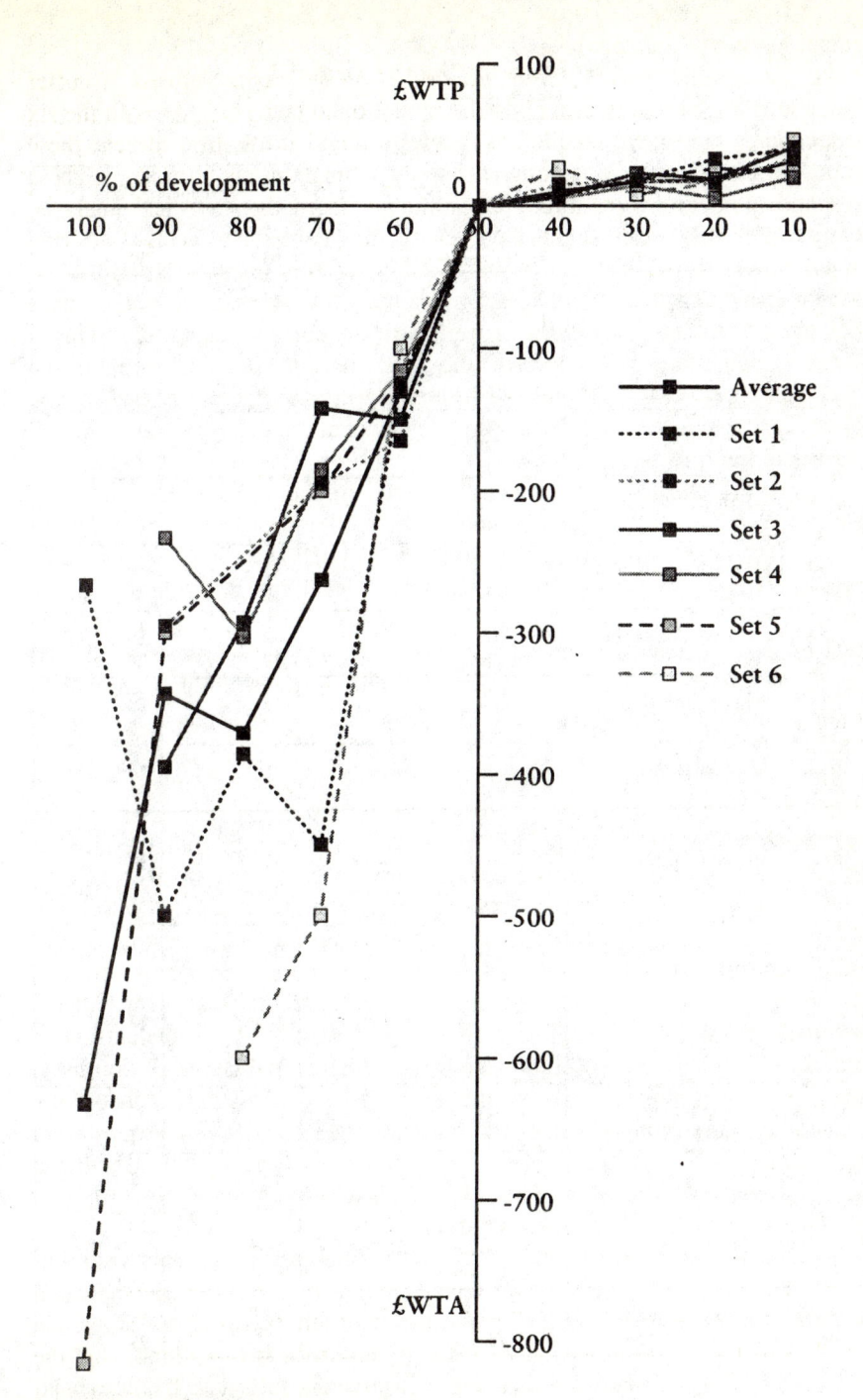

Figure 5.2: Survey 2 (N=291)

Table 5.1
Frequencies: Surveys 1 and 2

VARIABLE DESCRIPTION (Variable Label)	VALUES	SURVEY 1	SURVEY 2
		\multicolumn{2}{c}{Frequency (%)*}	
Living in the designated area (LIVIN)	0 = NO 1 = YES	37 63	5 95
Distance living away from the designated area (DIST)	0 = 0 miles 1 = < 2 miles 2 = 2 < 4 miles 3 = 4 - 6 miles 4 = > 6 miles	63 19 19 0 0	95 0 5 0 0
Users of green space in designated area (USE)	0 = NO 1 = YES	37 63	0 100
Used for walking (WALK)	0 = NO 1 = YES	44 56	5 95
Used for playing with children (PLAY)	0 = NO 1 = YES	81 19	65 35
Used for studying plants and animals (PLANTS)	0 = NO 1 = YES	62 38	80 20
Used for enjoying the views (VIEW)	0 = NO 1 = YES	56 44	30 70
Used for other purposes (OTHER)	0 = NO 1 = YES	75 25	100 0
Frequency of use of green space per month (FREQ)	0 = None 1 = 1 - 4 times 2 = 5 - 10 times 3 = More than 10 times	38 38 6 19	0 15 15 70
Enjoyment gained from green space (ENJOY)	0 = Low 5 = High	0 = 19 1 = 0 2 = 6 3 = 6 4 = 31 5 = 38	0 0 0 10 35 55
Knowledge of equivalent substitutes available (SUBS)	0 = NO 1 = YES	67 33	55 45
Household income group in £ p.a. (INC)	1 = < 10,000 2 = 10,000 - < 20,000 3 = 20,000 - < 30,000 4 = 30,000 - < 40,000 5 = 40,000 +	6 31 25 31 6	10 30 20 25 15
OK with payment method (METHOD)	0 = NO 1 = YES	13 88	5 95

* These frequencies are based on the number of respondents whose observations are used in the statistical analysis reported later, 16 for survey 1 and 20 for survey 2.

Given the contribution by Knetsch (1992), which suggests that the valuation curve may exhibit a 'kink' at the reference point, and upon reviewing the data illustrated in Figures 5.1 and 5.2, it was considered appropriate to use dummy variables in the regression analyses which become operative for WTA cases.

Although a cubic functional form such as

$$\text{VALUE} = a + b_1 X + b_2 X^2 + b_3 X^3, \qquad (5.2)$$

where X represents the percentage of green space under development, appears appropriate at first glance for survey 1, there is a distinct possibility of a Knetsch-type 'kink' appearing at the reference level of 50%, which would invalidate this form. Furthermore, the fact that the average curve in Figure 5.1 actually turns upwards as the amount of green space lost approaches 100% may be an anomaly requiring explanation rather than incorporation as part of the functional form. One explanation of this upward-sloping section is that respondents may have given up trying to save green space when faced with so little of it; for instance, some sort of threshold around 20% of green space left might have been applied and beyond this point they had little use for what was left. Perhaps, by then, the area would be too far to walk to, or the views from it, too mundane. It is also plausible that the upturn in Figure 5.1 is due solely to a statistical anomaly whereby these extreme cases were shown only to respondents who tended to require less than average compensation. This is especially relevant given the relatively small sample size. A final possible explanation is that the scenario of losing virtually all the green space in the area was considered implausible by respondents, who in turn gave ill-considered responses. As it is not known which, if any, of these explanations is the cause of this feature of the data, the correlations and results of the OLS multiple regressions for survey 1 exclude data points at the 80%, 90% and 100% levels, reducing the number of observations used in the statistical analysis of survey 1 to 177. This feature of the data for survey 1 was not replicated for survey 2, suggesting that the explanation based on there being a statistical anomaly may be most plausible. All data points were represented in the analysis for survey 2.

OLS was considered to be appropriate for this analysis given the lack of prior research in this field and, therefore, the lack of an *a priori* justification for the use of an alternative method such as weighted least squares (WLS). WLS, for instance, would be more appropriate if heteroscedasticity was anticipated, brought about, perhaps, by measurement error in the dependent variable increasing with the degree of change from the reference level. Use of WLS would place more weight on the more reliable aspects of the data. However, on *a priori* grounds, there appeared little justification for expecting substantial heteroscedasticity.

Variables included in the analyses of both surveys are listed below, along with the theoretical justifications for the inclusion of the various explanatory variables and the expected signs of their coefficients.

Dependent variable

The dependent variable is VALUE, which is simply the monetary amount that respondents gave as their (positive) WTP to save various amounts of green space or their (negative) WTA for losses of green space.

Explanatory variables

INC (measured on a scale 1 - 5) refers to the respondent's income group. The expected sign of its coefficient is positive as the higher the income, the greater the ability to pay given equal preferences. Although the relationship between income and WTP is likely to be positive, the expected functional form of the relationship is less clear. Each of the three functional forms, linear, logarithmic and quadratic, was tried. In each case, the coefficient on the income variable was not statistically different from zero, reinforcing the conclusions of the work of Bowker and MacDonald (1993) discussed earlier.

INCD is a dummy variable operative for WTA cases. The expected sign is negative reflecting the diminishing marginal utility of money. Higher income groups, it could be argued, would seek higher levels of compensation.

CENT (measured from 10% to 100%) represents the percentage of green space under development. The expected sign of its coefficient is negative as it is anticipated that respondents would be willing to pay more for fewer developments. As with INC, the appropriate functional form for this variable was not obvious on *a priori* grounds. If, for instance, there was a diminishing marginal utility derived from the green space, the natural logarithm of CENT would be the correct form. Again, a limited amount of exploration of the data was undertaken, which resulted in a simple linear form being adopted.[13]

---

[13] The testing of different functional forms for the regressors, as discussed with regard to INC and CENT, is one type of data mining and, as such, the number of degrees of freedom used in assessing statistical significance of the coefficients should be reduced accordingly. This follows the recommendation of Lovell (1983), whereby the degrees of freedom are reduced by the number of additional regressors tried. Lovell's rule of thumb is given by

$$\alpha = 1 - (1 - \hat{\alpha})^{c/k} \qquad (5.3)$$

CENTD is a dummy variable taking the value of one for WTA cases and zero otherwise. The discussion in Chapter 3 with regard to the divergence between WTP and WTA would support the expectation of a negative coefficient.

LIVIN was used as a variable to denote the respondent's home location. If a respondent lived in the planning area of the Bristol North Fringe, LIVIN took the value of one, and zero otherwise. A positive coefficient is expected.

LIVIND, operative for WTA cases, is expected to have a negative coefficient as those living in closer proximity to the green space would be expected to demand more in compensation.

SUBS is a binary variable equal to one if a respondent was aware of equivalent substitute facilities elsewhere and to zero otherwise. A negative coefficient is expected.

SUBSD is again a dummy variable taking the value of one for WTA cases, and zero otherwise. Given an expectation that those respondents who are aware of equivalent substitutes would demand less compensation, a positive sign is anticipated.

The level of detail on each map presented to respondents did not allow for all attributes (facilities) in the area to be listed or shown. As such, activities associated with the principal facilities were listed as proxies and respondents were asked to indicate whether or not they took part in those activities. Initial piloting of the questionnaire resulted in four principal activities being included in the survey. A variable OTHER was also used in order to allow for other activities to be included. All five 'activity' variables listed below are binary variables taking the value one if a respondent used the green space for that particular activity and zero otherwise. In all cases, the expected sign of the coefficient is positive. In order to explore whether an activity variable had a significantly different impact for WTA, a dummy variable was included for each activity variable. A negative coefficient is expected in each case.

---

where α is the true level of significance, $\hat{\alpha}$ is the calculated level and c and k represent the number of regressors considered and the number of regressors selected, respectively. Overall, given the relatively abundant degrees of freedom at the outset and the small amount of data mining undertaken, the effect on significance testing reported here would be to reduce marginally the significance of each regressor.

WALK: used for walking; also WALKD for WTA observations.

PLAY: used for playing with children; also PLAYD for WTA observations.

PLANTS: used for enjoying plants and animals; also PLANTSD for WTA observations.

VIEW: used for enjoying the views; also VIEWD for WTA observations.

OTHER: any other use for the green space; also OTHERD for WTA observations.

The variables listed above were used in the regression analyses. To examine internal consistency, a matrix of simple correlations of non-binary variables was calculated for each survey. VALUE, INC and two other variables (not listed above) were used. The two other variables were ENJOY, representing the level of a respondent's enjoyment gained from the area, and FREQ, determined by a respondent's frequency of use of the green space.

Table 5.2
Simple Correlations: Surveys 1 and 2

SURVEY 1 (N = 177)				
	VALUE	FREQ	ENJOY	INC
VALUE	1.00			
FREQ	-0.02	1.00		
ENJOY	-0.13	0.66**	1.00	
INC	0.08	-0.09	-0.45**	1.00
SURVEY 2 (N = 291)				
	VALUE	FREQ	ENJOY	INC
VALUE	1.00			
FREQ	0.21**	1.00		
ENJOY	0.04	0.61**	1.00	
INC	0.02	0.26**	0.06	1.00

Notes: ** denotes significance at the 0.1% level using a one-tailed test.

Prior to analysing the simple correlations, the r_{ij}, a number of points relating to the figures in Table 5.2 need to be addressed. First, it should be borne in mind that, to measure the magnitude of collinearity r_{ij}^2 should be considered. Furthermore, it is impossible from these figures to identify any hidden multicollinearity arising from relationships among more than two variables. Lastly, the signs on the coefficients in the VALUE column may well be different in the later regression analyses as a result of using multiple regression rather than simple correlations.

The first observation from the data presented in Table 5.2 is the lack of evidence supporting a hypothesis of strong internal consistency for either survey. The expectation was that both FREQ and ENJOY would exhibit a strong positive correlation with VALUE. Only in survey 2 is there some evidence of this, and here, even though the correlation coefficient is significant at the 0.1% level, the magnitude of association is relatively small ($0.21^2 = 0.044$). These coefficients, however, represent simple rather than partial correlations and there may well be a problem of *ceteris non paribus*. Reassuringly, in both surveys, the correlation coefficient for FREQ with ENJOY is significant and has the expected positive sign. Two other coefficients are significant although both indicate relatively small magnitudes of association. First, in survey 1, the negative correlation coefficient for ENJOY with INC suggests that those on lower incomes tend to gain the most enjoyment from the green space. This could be explained by those on higher incomes seeing local green space as an inferior good when compared to other facilities within easy driving distance. This relationship is not confirmed in the second survey, however. Furthermore, the correlation coefficient for FREQ with INC is positive and significant. This too provides a contradictory message. For survey 1 there is negative association between ENJOY and INC and, for survey 2, positive association between FREQ and INC. Given the substantiated expectation of positive association between FREQ and ENJOY, this apparent contradiction is difficult to explain. However, whilst there is little evidence in support of the hypothesis of strong internal consistency, there is no evidence to the contrary.

Table 5.3 contains the results of various regressions for surveys 1 and 2. Although the constant term in a simple regression can be interpreted as the intercept, in a multiple regression this is not the case. Each of the activity variables, for example, shifts the whole function either upwards (for example, VIEW in Equation (1)), or downwards (for example, WALK in Equation (3)). Any examination of the constant term's sign is thus meaningless in this context and is not dwelt upon here. The ensuing discussion of the coefficients in Table 5.3 takes place under the assumption of *ceteris paribus*.

Table 5.3
Regression Results: Surveys 1 and 2

Variable	Survey 1: Dependent Variable = VALUE (1)	(2)	Survey 2: Dependent Variable = VALUE (3)	(4)
CENT	-9.90*	-10.42	-14.18**	-13.67
CENTD	-117.34***	-121.22	-65.85***	-64.98
LIVIN	-5.67	-	-93.35#	-75.66
LIVIND	-18.82	-	-121.58**	-130.79
INC	-5.50	-	4.38	-
INCD	218.11***	215.88	-64.33***	-68.27
SUBS	-11.50	-	-22.92	-
SUBSD	-71.32	-	-162.29***	-176.02
WALK	-23.49	-	-140.69#	-148.80
WALKD	-2.38	-	482.52###	484.55
PLAY	1.96	-	3.99	-
PLAYD	-356.08**	-457.44	-48.10	-
PLANTS	0.93	-	-3.00	-
PLANTSD	679.69###	695.81	171.20###	156.01
VIEW	24.80	-	-3.58	-
VIEWD	-399.42***	-371.60	250.42###	260.63
OTHER	7.24	-	-	-
OTHERD	-596.55***	-599.24	-	-
R^2	80.2%	79.2%	69.0%	68.6%
$\bar{R}^2$	0.780	0.783	0.672	0.675
N	177	177	291	291

Notes: All F statistics are significant at the 0.1% level. Variables not included in the relevant regressions are denoted by '-'. Significance testing has not been carried out for Equations (2) and (4) as the significance of these variables has already been established from Equations (1) and (3) respectively. As none of the respondents in survey 2 indicated 'other' activity, OTHER and the associated dummy variable, OTHERD, were not included in equations (3) and (4). Using a one-tailed test, *, ** and *** denote significance at the 10%, 1% and 0.1% levels, respectively. Using a two-tailed test, #, ## and ### denote significance at the 10%, 1% and 0.1% levels, respectively.

Equations (1) and (3) represent the fully specified models for surveys 1 and 2, respectively. Equations (2) and (4) provide the results of simplified models using only the significant variables from Equations (1) and (3), respectively. If the excluded variables, from Equation (1) for example, were truly not relevant, then the coefficients of the included variables in Equation (2) should not be noticeably different from their counterparts in Equation (1). Indeed, this appears to be the case for both surveys. A comparison of the results from surveys 1 and 2, in terms of the likely success of benefit transfer, is discussed later.

The most striking observation from the results for Equation (1) is the absence of a statistically significant coefficient on many of the explanatory variables relating to WTP. Only the coefficient on CENT is significant at the 10% level. The negative sign on CENT's coefficient is as expected, people exhibit a WTP to save green space from developments, and the size of this coefficient suggests a rate of approximately £10 p.a. per 10% of green space saved. Given that the size of the green space within the designated area is approximately 6 km^2, this corresponds to an annual household willingness to pay to preserve green space of around £15 per km^2. All the other non-dummy variables (LIVIN, INC, SUBS, and the five activity variables) have coefficients which are not statistically different from zero. This suggests that, when it comes to paying, people are primarily concerned with the green space itself, not the use that is made of it. The results also suggest that a respondent's level of income and place of residence, either close by or in the designated area, are not significant determinants of WTP. The overall result for the WTP part of the data suggests that a very simple model, including a single variable representing only the amount of development in an area, may be sufficient for policy makers. If this is the case, and bearing in mind that this result may be solely attributable to INC being a poorly specified variable, it also suggests that green space in poorer, more densely populated areas holds a greater total social value than equivalent green space in more affluent, less densely populated areas.

Where respondents sought compensation (WTA), a very different and more complex picture emerges. In interpreting these results, the coefficient on the dummy variable should be added to that on the relevant non-dummy variable. For instance, the coefficient on PLAYD, Equation (1) of -356.08 should be added to PLAY's coefficient, 1.96. As PLAY's coefficient represents the amount by which the whole function would be shifted, the aggregated coefficients of PLAY and PLAYD also represent a shift of the whole function. The coefficient on CENTD takes the expected negative sign, highlighting the existence of a kink in the valuation function at the reference point. This confirms the findings discussed in Chapter 3, that for equivalent increments or decrements around a reference point, WTA tends to be greater than WTP. INCD's coefficient takes an unexpected positive sign, implying that those on higher incomes require relatively less in compensation. Whilst this conflicts with a rationale that the diminishing marginal utility of money would cause greater compensation to be demanded by those on higher incomes, such a result is consistent with the explanation given with regard to the simple correlation of INC with ENJOY, -0.45. If those on higher incomes regard local green space as an inferior good, it should be expected that they demand less in compensation.

The coefficients on the dummy activity variables, PLAYD, VIEWD and OTHERD, all take the expected negative sign, supporting the hypothesis that if green space is used for any of these activities then greater compensation will be sought. However, the size of each of these coefficients relative to that on CENTD suggests that these variables have a dominant influence on the total amount of compensation demanded. The coefficients on the variables LIVIND and SUBSD, and on the dummy activity variable WALKD, are not significantly different from zero.

PLANTSD causes some concern. This variable's coefficient takes an unexpected positive sign and is highly significant, at the 0.1% level, using a two-tailed test. At first glance, there does not seem to be an obvious explanation for this anomaly. The results suggest that those who enjoy the area for looking at plants and animals will reduce their demand for compensation by around £680. However, two explanations may be considered. First, it is possible, given the small sample size, that this result occurred by chance. The second, and equally plausible explanation, is based on mis-specification bias. Mis-specification bias could be due either to an omitted variable or to the inclusion of a variable where the wrong functional form has been specified. The theoretical justification of the functional forms for each of the included variables has already been examined and, therefore, is dismissed as the likely cause of this result. This leaves the case of an omitted variable to be examined. The most likely error here is the reliance on a single, crude measurement of income as a proxy for socio-economic characteristics. Indeed, this may have created an additional problem in that there is some measurement error associated with the income variable. Much of the potential variability of this variable was lost by forcing respondents to locate their household income within one of five income groups. Over ninety percent of responses fell within three of these five groups, thus further reducing the potential variability. As INC was the only socio-economic proxy used in this research the model had very limited ability to reflect the potential richness of attitudes towards this environmental good. However, in terms of mis-specification bias, if those enjoying the area for looking at plants and animals were generally less materialistic than others in the sample, then a reduction in compensation demanded would be expected. Using the income variable to represent socio-economic characteristics will obviously be inefficient in picking up such a trait. Where the omitted variable is both highly correlated with PLANTSD and highly relevant as a determinant of VALUE, the overall effect could be to change the sign on the included variable, in this case PLANTSD. If the omitted variable were one representing a socio-economic characteristic not captured by the income variable, then use of a richer, composite variable depicting 'lifestyle', such as ACORN, would no doubt have produced better results. It is possible that the omitted variable would have illustrated that that those who use the area for enjoying plants and animals tend to under-represent their required compensation or, for some good reason, give lower valuations than others in the sample.

Excluding the non-significant variables from Equation (1) provides little improvement in the explanatory power of the model, as evidenced by the results for Equation (2). $\overline{R}^2$ increases from 0.780 to 0.783, suggesting that the omitted variables had little explanatory power. The same is true of the results for the second survey where the exclusion of the non-significant variables again yields a very small rise in $\overline{R}^2$ (0.672 to 0.675). Moreover, the stability of the remaining coefficients when these variables are dropped from the regression confirms both their redundancy and the absence of serious multicollinearity.

Equation (3), which contains the results for the fully specified model for survey 2, provides for some interesting comparisons with Equation (1). It appears that, in the second survey, the determinants of WTP include not only CENT as in Equation (1), but also LIVIN and WALK. However, the coefficients on LIVIN and WALK both take an unexpected negative sign. A review of the data provided an explanation for this result. As can be seen from the frequencies in Table 5.1, only one respondent in survey 2 lived outside the designated area and, similarly, only one respondent did not use the area for walking. These were respondents 27 and 38, both of whom tended to give relatively high WTP figures. This suggests that the small sample size used in both surveys may be the cause of some of the apparently strange results. If LIVIN and WALK were to be ignored in the results for survey 2, the only determinant of WTP would be CENT, as for survey 1. The picture for WTA (compensation) is, once more, far more complex than for WTP, although the structure of this complexity in Equation (3) is strikingly different from that for Equation (1). Unlike Equation (1), in Equation (3) the coefficients on LIVIND, SUBSD and WALKD are significant and that on PLAYD is not significant. The coefficients on the other variables retain their level of significance between Equations (1) and (3), apart from OTHERD which was not represented in survey 2. However, in Equation (3), three out of the four included activity variables have coefficients which are significantly different from zero and take an unexpected positive sign. The explanations considered previously in relation to PLANTSD (Equation (1)) based on sample size and mis-specification bias, may also be applied here.

Figure 5.3 shows the average curves generated by the data for surveys 1 and 2.

In terms of the potential for benefit transfer (BT), Chow's test was applied to the pooled data from both surveys. Not suprisingly, given the differences between Equations (1) and (3) discussed above, the results of this test do not lend any support to the hypothesis that the whole demand function generated by survey 1 (Equation (1)) would be transferable to survey 2. However, the discrepancies between Equations (1) and (3) appear to relate to the determinants of VALUE where compensation was sought rather than where respondents exhibited a WTP to save green space. This is especially true if the arguments presented previously with regard to the spurious significance on the coefficients on LIVIN and WALK in Equation (3) are accepted. Furthermore, the size of the (significant) coefficients on CENT from surveys 1 and 2, -9.90 and -14.18, respectively,[14] along with their respective standard errors (4.98 and 8.31) suggests that, whilst both coefficients are significantly different from zero, they are not statistically different from one another. Thus a CVM, WTP-based format may be a usable platform for BT in this planning context. This finding coincides with that of Bergland *et al.* (1995), who found that they could not reject the hypothesis of the transferability of estimated per household benefits for water quality improvement. They did, however, find grounds for rejecting the hypothesis of the transferability of the complete benefit function.

In addition to using the socio-economic characteristics employed in the analyses discussed above, an alternative specification of the model was tried whereby each respondent, apart from the first in each survey, was represented by a dummy variable. These dummy variables were then included in the analyses of the data for each survey, along with CENT and CENTD, in an attempt to identify groups (or individuals) who tended to give valuations which were significantly different from the first respondent in

---

[14] These coefficients, derived from surveys conducted two years apart, should be adjusted by a compound inflation figure of approximately 5-6%. This would make the coefficients even more similar than is portrayed above. It is also true that a significant building project commenced during the two-year gap between the surveys which, as it met with sizeable opposition from residents in the area, may have influenced some of the valuations in survey 2.

It should also be remembered that the two surveys were conducted using different modes of interaction between interviewer and respondent. The implications of using a computer-based application for survey 1 and a face-to-face mode for survey 2 were not explored, even though it is likely that this change would have produced some distortion in the results.

each survey. However, the coefficients on these dummy variables were difficult to interpret meaningfully as they were generated using both positive (WTP) and negative (WTA) valuations. Thus, any interpretation could not distinguish where a respondent gave a significantly different WTP but a similar WTA, or vice versa. For instance, the valuations given by respondent 6 were significantly different from those of respondent 1 (and, by implication, significantly different from other respondents in survey 1) with respondent 6 seemingly tending to offer both a lower WTP and requiring a higher (more negative) WTA. Conversely, respondents 20 and 23 tended to offer significantly more than respondent 1 in terms of WTP and required significantly less in compensation. Similarly, in survey 2, respondents 28, 29, 34 and 39 apparently formed a group which tended to offer a significantly lower WTP and a higher WTA than did respondent 25. Respondents 35 and 38, on the other hand, appear to offer a significantly higher WTP and lower WTA when compared with respondent 25. A review of the data was conducted in order to see whether these groups of respondents shared similar characteristics in terms of the use made of the green space, level of enjoyment gained from the area, place of residence in relation to the green space, knowledge of substitute sites and income group. There were no discernable patterns. As an example, respondent 20 lived in the area, didn't use the green space, didn't enjoy the green space, was aware of substitute facilities and was in income group 2. Respondent 23 lived just outside of the designated area but nonetheless used the green space for walking and for the views, gaining a high level of enjoyment and was in income group 3. The only similarity with respondent 20 was that both knew of equivalent substitutes. The fact that these two respondents, and those in other groupings, tended to give similar valuations but did not exhibit any identifiable group characteristics would support the argument for use of more detailed socio-economic characteristics (such as ACORN) than was the case in these two surveys.

In an attempt to overcome this difficulty in interpretation, all but the first respondent in each survey were represented using two dummy variables. The first became operative where a particular respondent exhibited a WTP and the second becoming operative where that same respondent sought compensation. Difficulties arose in a number of cases where respondents valued only a small number of alternatives on either side of the reference point. Where there was no variation in these valuations, owing to these alternatives, quite by chance, representing similar levels of development, no coefficients could be generated. Where results were obtained, again a review of the socio-economic characteristics did not lead to any obvious determinants for the apparent groupings.

It would have been interesting also to have considered the pattern of responses given by each respondent throughout the valuation exercise.

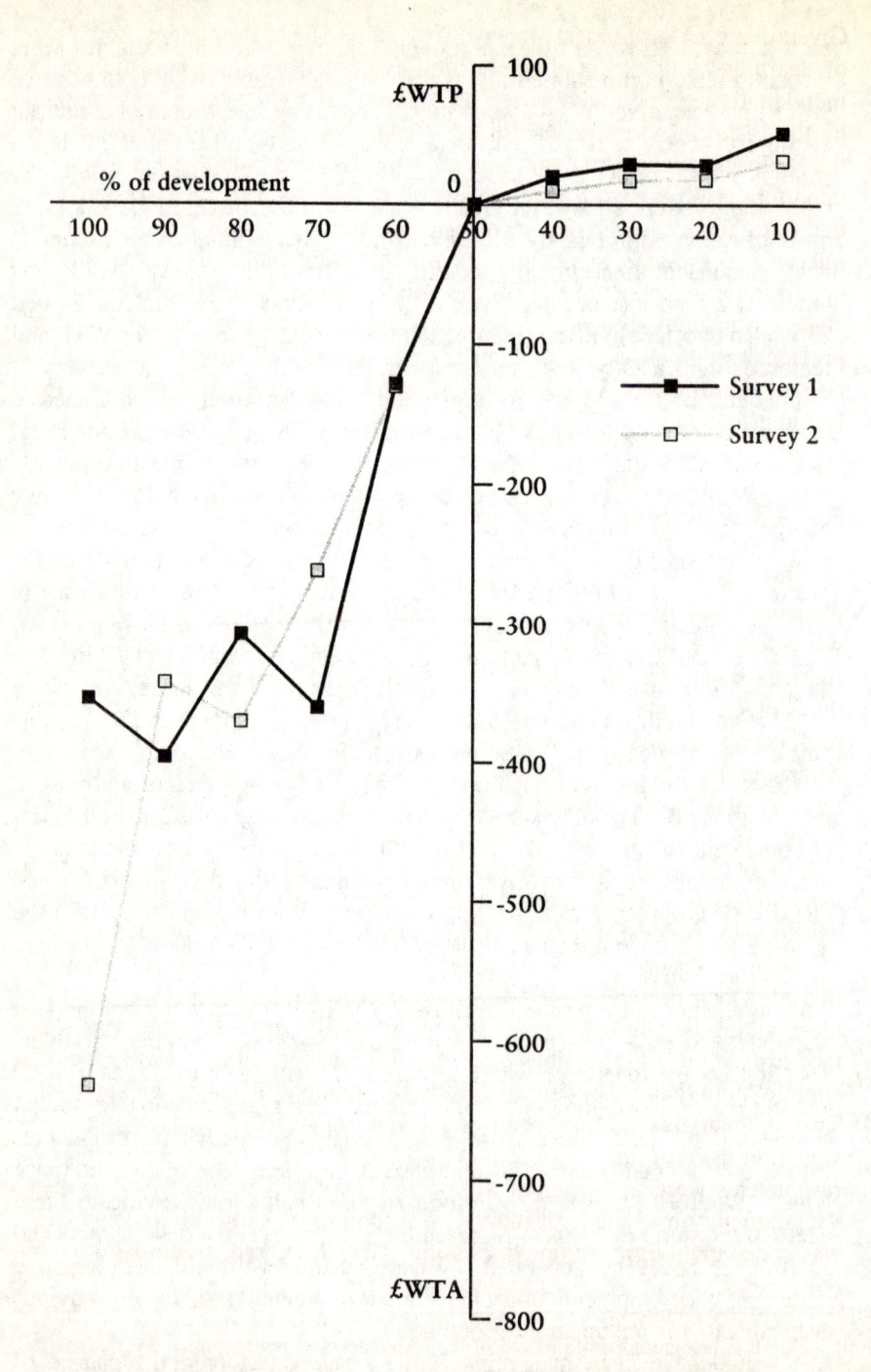

Figure 5.3: Averages; 1&2

Given that each respondent was asked to value 15 separate maps, some sort of 'learning by doing' might have been evidenced by an examination of an individual's responses. However, in order to satisfy the conditions imposed by the Fishbein-Ajzen model (discussed in Section 3.5.1.1) and especially the feedback mechanism explicit in their model, respondents were given the opportunity to review all fifteen valuations at the end of their session. As the first survey was conducted using interactive software, without an interviewer present, the extent to which respondents made use of this opportunity is unknown.[15] In the second survey, respondents did not always wait until the end of the interview to exercise their right to alter previous responses. Re-evaluation of responses was an on-going process and no record was kept of the extent of this activity. This suggests that some learning by doing was taking place.

5.4.1 The Respondents' Experience

As this work has sought to facilitate improved public participation in planning, it seemed appropriate to ask respondents about the approach which was adopted. Of sixteen respondents giving valid responses in survey 1, fourteen responded to a follow-up questionnaire. The remaining two had left the University and forwarding addresses were not known. The twenty respondents in survey 2 were all questioned immediately after they had completed the valuation exercise. The questionnaire (appendix 3) explored respondents' experiences of the current participation process and asked them to compare this with the approach adopted here.

Half of the respondents in the first survey thought that this proactive, valuation-based approach would lead to the public having a greater say in the development of local plans. Four respondents were indifferent and three, all of whom had successfully negotiated the existing processes in the past, indicated their preference for the status quo. A similar pattern is evident for those taking part in the second survey although, as these were conducted face-to-face, it was possible to gain additional insights. Here, twelve, slightly more than half, were in favour of adopting this valuation approach. Two did not like the approach at all and suggested that they found the valuation part of the approach extremely difficult. The remaining six respondents were in favour of a proactive approach but not one based on valuation nor on a sample of individual responses. Their preferred approach was one involving group discussion, which sounded similar to the

---

[15] It is recognized that a record of the respondents taking the opportunity to review their responses could have been built into the programme. This was an oversight which should be considered in future research.

participatory democracy approach advocated by, amongst others, Jacobs (1996). The number of respondents involved is obviously too small to draw any general conclusions from the results, but it is interesting to note how few respondents, three in fourteen in survey 1 and only one in twenty in survey 2, had any experience at all of the current participation process.

5.5 Conclusions and Shortcomings

Given that the primary objective of this research has been to provide an aid to the public participation process, the results presented in Sections 5.4 and 5.4.1 offer some encouragement.

It appears that respondents are able to deal with hypothetical representations of developments of existing green space within a defined planning area. Also, the use of a hypothetical reference level worked well, as is evidenced by all valid responses lying in the north-east or south-west quadrants of Figures 5.1 and 5.2. However, given some of the problems highlighted in the analyses of cases of compensation, it might be most fruitful to rely on a model of WTP to preserve green space using the current level of development as the reference point. This would negate the need to use a hypothetical reference point at all.

Reassuringly, the average bids depicted in Figure 5.3 accord very closely with the theoretically based valuation curve shown and discussed in Chapter 3. Indeed, the WTA and WTP bids for equivalent decrements or increments are substantially different from one another.

In terms of the method of payment, the payment vehicle, via an independent management company, met with little protest and it may be deemed to be an appropriate mechanism for use in future research.

As stated throughout, the second aim of this research has been to explore the transferability of contingent valuation results between planning areas. Initially, it was suggested that a means of achieving this aim lay in the adoption of an 'attributes' approach to the valuation exercise. Owing to the difficulty of illustrating all the attributes in detail, activity proxies were used to ascertain which attributes were of most importance to respondents. The results of the two surveys indicate that this approach may have been superfluous. It was discussed in the analysis of the results that perhaps only one explanatory variable, that representing the amount of proposed development, would be necessary if the WTP format were to be adopted. The WTA format produced numerous unexpected results which were not replicated between surveys and, accordingly, it was recommended that this approach be avoided. Use of the simple WTP model also led to the conclusion that BT had some potential in this planning context.

As alluded to above, a limitation of this work has been the inability to represent in detail the attributes within the planning area. This was largely due to the nature of the available software and the necessary complexity of the representations. This may have led to some ambiguities in the respondents' interpretations of the proposed changes. In future research of this type, much greater detail of changes should be given to respondents, either graphically, verbally or in writing. The work of Collins *et al.* (1993), in using 3-D modelling and interactive media, may provide insights here.

A second shortcoming has been the reliance on the use of an 'income' variable to represent socio-economic characteristics. Although not proven here, it is suggested that the use of income may be inferior to the use of other variables such as the composite 'lifestyle' classifications which are commercially available e.g. ACORN. In many ways these composite variables take account of income, although this is then supplemented with the type of lifestyle chosen by an individual. It is this important supplementary element which can shed light on the likelihood of a respondent's being, say, materialistic or otherwise. Furthermore, composite lifestyle variables are likely to give some insight into the reason why protest votes are received. The 25% protest votes in survey 1 and around 17% for survey 2 were from (non)respondents across the whole range of incomes. It is suggested that further detail of socio-economic characteristics would shed more light on the determinants of protest votes.

6 Summary and Conclusions

6.0 Introduction

The general public's views on the shape and pace of developments in their localities are still being inadequately accounted for by planners. Planners are heavily reliant on participation procedures which predate the recent important developments in survey-based techniques, including valuation techniques and notably the contingent valuation method (CVM). If their reluctance to accept survey-based methods is founded on cost grounds, this can be challenged on two fronts. First, cost should be compared with the effectiveness of any participation procedure in relation to its objective. If people's views are being overlooked, then current expenditure on public participation is wasteful. Secondly, through the practice of benefit transfer, it should be possible to minimize the costs associated with survey-based valuations.

The planning literature reviews and analyses different approaches to the process of public participation but invariably these approaches represent incremental changes to current practice. A significant departure from current practice is recommended here. It is argued that a cost-effective route to a proactive form of public participation is viable.

6.1 Public Participation - Current Practice

In 1969 the Skeffington Report concluded that the general public should be more involved in the process of development of their locality. In essence, the authors of the Report recommended that planners should introduce facilitating techniques and processes that would enable such involvement. In Chapter 2, the main attempts at facilitation were reviewed. It was shown there that public inquiry procedures, the principal vehicles for public participation according to Alty and Darke (1989), were inadequate, using overly complex language and inappropriate timing. Where help was given to community groups, through such programmes as Community Technical Aid, the degree of commitment by planners and government was open to question. Minimal budgets were allocated to such schemes, for example. A review of case studies, notably those by Webster and Lavers (1991), Alty and Darke (1989) and Blackman (1991b) also suggested that public participation procedures did not meet the goal of extensive participation. These studies were concerned with the success, or otherwise, of programmes designed to facilitate public participation. Alty and Darke, for example, in their review of the 1986 Sheffield experience, found that even where extensive public participation had taken place, there were inadequate resources applied to abstracting, summarizing and disseminating the findings. Blackman highlighted the subjective criteria applied to the arguments of different groups of respondents. As a means of measuring success in these case studies, the findings were compared with Arnstein's (1969) 'Ladder of Participation'. At best, it seems that the current processes of public participation might be labelled as 'window dressing'.

In order to test the conclusions drawn from the review of public participation using secondary data, a questionnaire was sent to all Chief Planning Officers in England and Wales. A response rate approaching 70% was achieved. The results of this survey substantiate the hypothesis that public participation procedures are inadequate when measured against the objectives espoused in the Skeffington Report. The principal findings from the survey revealed that there is no evidence that planners have taken a proactive stance to gaining responses from individuals to a proposed plan. Whilst legal requirements were satisfied by the use of newspaper advertisements detailing the proposal (or at least where it might be viewed), responses were not sought at an individual level in any proactive way. The philosophy was one of legal compliance, not active elicitation of preferences. Individuals were encouraged to respond either through a community group or by submitting written responses, but proposals were not taken to the public, rather the public had to seek out the proposals themselves. Furthermore, forms available from planners, provided for the public to submit comments on a plan, did not allow for intensity of feeling to be communicated in any objective manner. Although the figure varied, depending on the development stage of the plan, around 15% of planners suggested that intensity of feeling was gauged purely by the number of responses received. In other cases, subjective appraisal of a written submission was recognised as the normal procedure for gauging intensity of feeling. Such a procedure, where junior and middle-ranking planners seek, without guidelines, to interpret the importance of a response, will obviously be prone to unequal consideration being given across all responses. Even if local guidance is available, the absence of any national procedures would result in inter-regional inequalities. Indeed, from the planners' responses, intensity of feeling was deemed '.... not a material planning consideration'. Returning to Dasgupta and Pearce's (1972) statement that:

> The town planner, for example, is frequently without any systematic criteria, save his own paternalistic preferences. (p 15)

this is an unsatisfactory state of affairs, suggesting that little improvement has taken place over the last twenty years.

The problems outlined above are further compounded by the lack of representation of some socio-economic and ethnic groups in the process. Around 50% of planners indicated that, in their view, responses were not received from a wide enough cross-section of the general public.

More alarmingly, over 90% of planners who responded stated that public participation resulted in 'minor' or 'no changes' to the proposed plan. This suggests that either planners tend to get it right first time or that the current process of public participation is ineffective. The review of the secondary data and the results of the survey would suggest that the latter is the case.

6.2 Potential Improvements

There is no easy solution to the problems encountered by planners when they seek to assess individuals' preferences. Arrow's (1951) contribution in this area culminated in his impossibility theorem which, because of his rejection of interpersonal comparisons based on measures of cardinal utility, considered the necessary conditions for a successful ordinal approach to the task. The fact that no voting scheme fulfils all of Arrow's conditions is documented in a recent review by Levin and Nalebuff (1995) and is acknowledged by Sen (1995).

However, two broad strategic changes to the participation process might be considered. First, consideration could be given to an extension and improvement of systems of representative democracy such as the Community Technical Aid scheme or of the developing theory of participatory democracy (Jacobs (1996)). Secondly, and forming the basis of the recommendations here, planners might look to extending direct democracy. The second solution is not new to planners. Surveys, for example, have been a part of the planning process since the early Geddesian (1915) model was formulated. However, it is the relatively recent advances in survey-based methods, and in economic valuation in particular, which prompt the recommendation that planners reconsider this approach. Instead of focusing on macro level demographic and economic indicators which were characteristic of the early planning surveys, the advances in survey techniques and data handling now offer the opportunity to consider micro level data. The idea of using surveys is itself not new to planners but the use of surveys to elicit and measure individual preferences is a significant departure from current practice. However, even such a significant change should not be seen as radical. Proactive consultation at the individual level, on a sample basis, is proposed in order to supplement rather than supplant current procedures. Of course, supplementary procedures introduced in a financially constrained environment will compete for scarce responses. This suggests that a strong rationale is needed where new procedures are recommended to replace old ones. Two requirements should be considered. First, the effectiveness of the recommended procedure should be compared with existing procedures given the objective of facilitating public participation. Secondly, the proposed procedure should be cost-effective. Where a recommended procedure meets the former, this might result in some marginal changes in resources allocated to different procedures, as more efficient techniques replace some current practice. Achieving the latter requirement, however, is seen as essential in overcoming resistance from a planning profession which is financially constrained. Thus, the requirement is for a procedure which could elicit the preferences of the general public about some plan, gauge the intensity of those preferences, and which could do so at an acceptable cost.

It should be borne in mind that survey-based solutions to any problem can be expensive. A significant proportion of this expense can be allocated to the actual fieldwork for an interviewer's time and expenses. If such expense could be avoided, or at least reduced, a CVM-type survey approach to capturing the publics' intensity of preference would be more likely to be acceptable to planners. Thus, an important theme here has been the design of a procedure which would facilitate the transfer of results between localities and, therefore, between plans. This 'preference transfer' or 'benefit transfer' (BT) would obviate the need for original surveys to be undertaken each time a plan is proposed.

However, there is a trade-off which needs to be considered. One of the proposed benefits of a proactive approach to participation lies in the increased involvement of the public in the decision-making process, but the greater the success of BT, the less is the need for that proactive involvement. This balance would need careful thought and would probably be determined by the specific context of a proposed development, especially the scale of those developments and the anticipated consequences.

Section 3.6 and Chapter 4, (BT) and factorial survey design (FSD), respectively, were combined to provided the basis of a framework for developing BT in this planning context. Stewart's (1983) model of individual choice, along with Lancaster's (1966) attribute theory, suggest that choice between plans would be determined by the attributes offered by each of the plans. This attribute approach formed the basis of a model of BT which achieves the objectives of affordability and cost-effectiveness. BT was reviewed in terms of its historical development and in terms of its theoretical basis. Where there is a need for accurate measures of welfare change, the usefulness of BT declines. However, where indicative measures would suffice, BT was deemed to be a useful and cost-effective mechanism. Chapter 4 illustrated how the use of FSD, in conjunction with the CVM, could elicit intensity of preference for various attributes.

In Chapter 3, an extensive review of the CVM was presented. It was found that, whilst contributing a significant advance in the theory of economic valuation, this technique is not without problems. For example, embedding effects, where consideration of an entity gives a significantly lower total value than if subcomponents of that entity are valued independently and then summed, was seen as a major issue. This was overcome here, to some extent, by respondents being presented with total entities (plans) for valuation. By altering the level of attributes in the plans, multiple regression analysis was used to estimate the contribution to total value of each of the attributes.

In addition to its ability to encompass nonuse, as well as use, values, the CVM was also shown to produce measures of Hicksian consumer's surplus. This is known to be a more accurate indication of a change in an individual's welfare than the Marshallian measures produced using the travel cost approach or hedonic pricing. Whilst this illustrates an advantage of the CVM over competing valuation techniques it is also an area concerning the use of the CVM which has generated much debate. For example, where a welfare loss is being considered, the correct Hicksian measure would be the compensating surplus associated with willingness to accept (WTA). However, the review of the CVM in Chapter 3 illustrated the wide disparities which researchers have found between WTA and WTP (willingness to pay). This debate has been resolved only in a practical sense. Users of the CVM have been encouraged to use WTP, rather than WTA, as the results can then be interpreted as conservative estimates of the change in an individual's welfare and are thus more likely to be acceptable to policy makers. This divergence between WTP and WTA was a key feature of the results presented in Chapter 5, with the relative conservatism of WTP clearly evident.

Sources of error in CVM-based estimates were also reviewed. The error was shown to affect either the reliability and or the validity of the estimates and the principal sources of error were reviewed under the two headings of researcher-based or respondent-based. It was concluded that these sources of error could be minimized by careful design of a CVM instrument. As an example, strategic behaviour by a respondent could be minimized by careful framing of the payment question. A respondent should be under the impression that provision of the public good in question would be dependent upon the values given by those in the sample, even though the actual level of payment by each individual remains uncertain at the time of the survey.

An extension of existing recommendations for the use of the CVM was discussed and it was argued that more care should be devoted to the rights of respondents. Where such rights are violated, it was suggested that unreliable results may ensue and, given a likely more extensive use of the CVM in the future, this could become a significant problem. For instance, respondents should be given the right to refuse to participate, the right to safety, such as the avoidance of stressful situations and deceptive practices, and the right to be informed of results. Many of these rights were already included in an early version of the code of conduct for the European Market Research Society, although they were omitted in that of the American Marketing Association. As the technique has been used and developed predominantly in the USA, its implementation in Europe and elsewhere may necessitate some changes to currently accepted practice.

In Chapter 2, the CVM was examined in relation to the need to weight valuation results due to differences in income between those affected in a cost-benefit study. It was hypothesised that the CVM results may already be weighted depending on the stance, public or private, taken by a respondent. This is undoubtedly an area for further research.

6.3 Principal Findings from the Fieldwork

The results presented in Chapter 5 suggest that the CVM could be used to enhance public participation in the development of local plans. Furthermore, the comparative analysis of the results of the two surveys suggests that BT might be possible in this planning context, especially where only indicative estimates of value are required. Supporting the conclusions drawn by Bergland *et al.* (1995), the analysis of the fieldwork suggests that a per household benefit of saving green space would be transferable. The results do not support the hypothesis of the transferability of the complete demand function.

The number of observations obtained for each survey was 360, representing 15 responses from each of 24 respondents, although, for the various reasons discussed in Chapter 5, the number of observations used in the statistical analysis of each survey fell to 177 and 291 respectively. There were three reasons for choosing a relatively small sample size. The first related to resource constraints, in terms of the incentives available to respondents, and the second reason, to the use of specialist technology in the first survey, which made it necessary to conduct the experiment at the University of the West of England. These two reasons determined the extent of the 'volunteer' population. The final reason relates to one of the objectives for the research, namely to investigate a cost-effective route to improving public participation. Thus it was deemed appropriate to examine the implications of using multiple responses from each respondent. The most likely adverse affect of such an approach would be autocorrelation where respondent's systematically overestimate or underestimate in their valuations of various plans. Apart from the few cases discussed in Chapter 5, there was no evidence that this had occurred. To some extent this is a promising result although further work using the same procedures is necessary before any final conclusion is drawn on this issue. However, undoubtedly the relatively small sample size has been one factor giving rise to some of the surprising results from the fieldwork.

The specialist technology used in the first survey consisted of a tailor-made programme which allowed graphical representations of plans to be shown to respondents. This programme also allowed information regarding the plans to be accessed by respondents and for their final valuations to be recorded. Use of this interactive software avoided interviewer bias but may have been the cause of sampling bias due to self-selection because of a fear of technology. In order to meet the requirements of a successful CVM-based survey and, also, to incorporate the factorial survey design approach, substantial effort was given to the design of the software. High quality graphics were achieved using the Genesis software package which also allowed for the random presentation of attributes to respondents. Various pilot stages were used to test the clarity and respondent understanding of the procedures. Upon reflection, given the specific hardware requirements for its operation, use of the Genesis package restricted the 'portability' of the survey. For future research, it may be necessary to trade-off graphics quality for portability, especially if the proactive survey approach, recommended here, is to be implemented.

Linked to the development of the software, it would be important that combinations of attributes are able to be shown, rather than the single attribute changes reported here. This would be more realistic and would address more closely the underlying theory of the factorial survey design method.

The second survey, conducted at Sainsbury's in the Bristol North Fringe planning area, involved the same high quality graphics, but this time, presented as hard copies to respondents. Apart from the obvious reintroduction of interviewer bias, it was felt that this was a satisfactory procedure.

The computer programme, whilst sophisticated in many respects, was unable to show adequate detail of each plan and thus the attributes had to be represented by activity variables. Where, for instance, a respondent indicated that the area in question was used for walking, it was anticipated that changes in the plans which inhibited this activity would be reflected in higher valuations. To some extent the results accord with this theoretical expectation. However, there were some surprising results. In Equation (4) in Table 5.3, for example, walkers were apparently willing to pay £140 less than those classifying themselves as non-walkers. Chapter 5 discussed the suggestion that this, rather than being surprising, may have been a true reflection of the WTP of walkers. It was suggested that walkers may be less materialistic than non-walkers and that the socio-economic proxy variable used, household income, was inadequate for identifying the life-style of respondents. In conjunction with the need to gain a better understanding of the determinants of protest votes, this provides a case for future research to incorporate composite socio-economic variables, such as the commercially available ACORN data.

As mentioned previously, it is also highly likely that the relatively small sample size contributed to some of the anomalies arising in the interpretation of the results. However, the results of the statistical analysis themselves are only secondary in importance to the concept of a proactive approach to public participation, the potential for which has been illustrated in this work. Given greater resources, further improvements would be possible, especially in the portrayal of plans to respondents and also in the use of the CVM. More resources would enable the statistically superior, dichotomous choice format to be adopted, which relies on a relatively large sample size. Nonetheless, some real evidence for the potential for this proactive, CVM-based approach came from the respondents themselves. Around two-thirds of respondents (22 out of 34) stated that they thought this approach would lead to the public having a greater say in the development of local plans. Given the conclusions from the analysis of public participation in Chapter 2, it was not surprising to find that only 4 respondents had had any experience of public participation processes in a local planning context.

6.4 Concluding Remarks

It is imperative that people 'own' the decisions which shape their environment. Ownership may engender stewardship and, in turn, sustainability. The use of preference elicitation in a proactive, survey approach to public participation, would undoubtedly widen the cross-section of those involved in the planning process. The CVM is, by its very nature, public participation.

APPENDIX 1 - Questionnaire to Chief Planning Officer
(see Chapter 2)

PUBLIC PARTICIPATION/CONSULTATION AT DISTRICT LEVEL

General Public Involvement in the Development of Local Plans

'General Public' should include organisations and local groups but not statutory consultees.

Q1 How are the *general public* informed of the participation/consultation exercise at each of the stages listed?

(please tick as appropriate : you may tick more than one box per stage)

	Public Informed by:					
STAGE	E	PM	N	T	R	Other (please specify)
Informal Consultation Draft						
Deposit Consultation						
Inquiry or Examination in Public						
Consultations on Modifications						

E (Exhibitions), PM (Public Meetings), N (Newspapers), T (Television), R (Radio)

Q2 Does every household receive a direct communciation about the participation exercise?   YES / NO

Q3 Which form of media is used to present the plan to the *general public* at each stage?

(please tick as appropriate : you may tick more than one box per stage)

STAGE	M	Eo	E	PM	N	T	V	R	Other (please specify)
Informal Consultation Draft									
Deposit Consultation									
Inquiry or Examination in Public									
Consultations on Modifications									

M   - Mail including leaflet drop or council newsletter with invitation to reply
PM - Public Meeting minuted
R   - Radio with invitation to reply
Eo - Exhibition with Officers, forms available for reply
N   - Newspaper with invitation to reply
V   - Video with invitation to reply
E   - Exhibition without officers, forms available for reply
T   - Television with invitation to reply

Q4 At each stage, how are the majority of responses from the *general public* received?

(please tick as appropriate : you may tick more than one box per stage if responses are equally split between 2 or more categories)

STAGE	ML	MF	P	C	Other (please specify)
Informal Consultation Draft					
Deposit Consultation					
Inquiry or Examination in Public					
Consultations on Modifications					

ML - Mail (non-official form), MF - Mail (official form), P - Telephone,
C - Notes from face-to-face conversation with officer

Q5   In your view, do you receive responses from a wide enough cross-section of the *general public* at each stage?

(please circle as appropriate)

STAGE	
Informal Consultation Draft	YES / NO
Deposit Consultation	YES / NO
Inquiry or Examination in Public	YES / NO
Consultations on Modifications	YES / NO

Q6   How is the *general public's* intensity of feeling towards any aspect of the plan calculated at each stage?

(please tick one box per stage)

STAGE	1. no. of responses	2. tone of responses	3. status of respondents	4. Quality of response	5. Some Combination of 1,2,3,4	6. Other (please specify
Informal Consultation Draft						
Deposit Consultation						
Inquiry or Examination in Public						
Consultations on Modifications						

If you wish to provide further comment on this question please do so here:

....
....

Q7   In your view, are some community or commerical groups given more than average opportunity to participate?   YES / NO

Q8   If 'yes' to Q7, which sector(s) in particular?

....

Q9   In your view, how much importance is given to the preferences of the *general public* at each stage?

(please tick one box per stage)

STAGE	Significant	Some	Little	Very Little	None
Informal Consultation Draft					
Deposit Consultation					
Inquiry or Examination in Public					
Consultations on Modifications					

Q10   In your view, is the importance given at each stage in Q9 adequate?

(please circle as appropriate)

STAGE	
Informal Consultation Draft	YES / NO
Deposit Consultation	YES / NO
Inquiry or Examination in Public	YES / NO
Consultations on Modifications	YES / NO

Q11 If you answered 'No' to any part of Q10, what is (are) the major constraint(s) you face in attempting to improve this process?

(please tick as appropriate, you may tick more than one box per stage)

STAGE	Public Apathy	Financial	Statutory	Staffing	LA Policy/ Culture	Other (please specify)
Informal Consultation Draft						
Deposit Consultation						
Inquiry or Examination in Public						
Consultations on Modifications						

Q12 On the whole, has public participation led to:

(please circle the appropriate number)

<u>Many major</u> revisions to local plan?   1

<u>Few major</u> revisions to local plan?   2

<u>Many minor</u> revisions to local plan?   3

<u>Few minor</u> revisions to local plan?   4

No revisions to local plan?   5

If you would like to add any comments about your views of the public participation process please do so here.

. . . .

. . . .

. . . .

Many thanks for your co-operation.

If you would like to receive a summary of these results free of charge, please tick this box ☐ and add your name and address below:

Name: ....

Position: ....

Work address: ....

....

....

Tel no: ....

There may be the opportunity to conduct in-depth case study follow-ups on some district's responses. If you would be willing to participate in this process please tick this box ☐ and ensure the address section above is complete.

All responses will remain confidential.

APPENDIX 2 - Background Information and Questionnaire
(see Chapter 5)

First of all, welcome and many thanks for agreeing to take part in this research exercise.

We would like to put your mind at rest by stating at the outset that all your responses given in this exercise will remain totally confidential. As we are hoping that Northavon Planning Department will be interested in the results, they will only be given averages and no individual responses will be identifiable.

There are no right or wrong answers in this exercise. What we are looking for are your values for certain combinations of proposed developments and green space which may occur in the North Fringe Planning Area.

Please follow carefully the instructions which will be given to you as you move through the exercise.

When you are ready to begin, just click the left-hand button on the mouse after moving the on-screen arrow to the 'NEXT' box in the bottom right corner. After completing a simple questionnaire, you will be shown a map of the whole of the North Fringe Planning Area before focusing then on a small part of it for the rest of the exercise.

QUESTIONNAIRE

All responses will remain confidential

PLEASE ENTER YOUR 3 FIGURE SAMPLE NUMBER HERE _ _ _

1. Do you live within the bounded area shown on the first map?

    1 = YES   0 = NO   If 'YES' GO TO Q2, if 'NO' GO TO Q3

2. Do you live within the bounded area shown on the second map?

    1 = YES   0 = NO   GO TO Q4

3. How far away from the area do you live?

    1 = under 2 miles

    2 = 2 - 4 miles

    3 = 4 - 6 miles

    4 = over 6 miles

4. Do you have any use at all for the green space depicted on the second map?

    1 = YES   0 = NO   If 'NO' GO TO Q7

5. What activity or activities do you use this green space for?

    a) WALKING   1 = YES   0 = NO

    b) PLAYING WITH CHILDREN   1 = YES   0 = NO

    c) LOOKING AT PLANTS OR ANIMALS   1 = YES   0 = NO

    d) THE VIEWS   1 = YES   0 = NO

    e) OTHER USE NOT MENTIONED ABOVE   1 = YES   0 = NO

6. Approximately, how often do you make any use of this green space in a month?

   1 = LESS THAN 5 TIMES PER MONTH

   2 = 5 - 10 TIMES PER MONTH

   3 = MORE THAN 10 TIMES PER MONTH

7. Overall, how would you rate the level of enjoyment you derive from this green space?

   HIGH   LOW

   5 4 3 2 1 0

8. If the whole of the green space was replaced with developments are you aware of equivalent alternatives you could use? In answering, you should bear in mind the enjoyment you would get from these alternatives, and the ease of getting to them, relative to the existing green space.

   1 = YES 0 = NO

9. Because you will be asked to compare various different maps using money as a measurement, it would be helpful if you would indicate your approximate *household* income.

   0 = I do not wish to answer this question

   1 = LESS THAN £10,000

   2 = £10,000 to £19,999

   3 = £20,000 to £29,999

   4 = £30,000 to £39,999

   5 = OVER £40,000

10. Given that an organisation may be set up to protect the level of green space chosen by yourself and others, it will need to receive money from you or make payments to you depending upon the final level chosen. Do you have any objection to this organisation being independent of government and of charitable status?

    1 = YES   0 = NO   If 'NO' GO TO END

11. Would you prefer the organisation to be controlled by:

    1 = Central Government?

    2 = Local Government?

    3 = Private sector?

    4 = Some other not mentioned above?

END - THANK YOU - We will now move on to the valuation exercise.

You have already seen a map showing the whole North Fringe Planning Area and another focusing on an area of green space towards the eastern edge of the area as it is currently. For the rest of this exercise we will be dealing only with this more focused area.

As you move on from this point you will be asked to consider pairs of maps. The first to be shown each time will be a reference map depicting 50% of the current green space given up to either housing, light industry/business or retail developments and the second in the pair will be a variation, say 70% or, perhaps, 30% of green space gone. The '50%' reference maps may show either blocks of green space being developed or the developments may be scattered throughout the area.

GIVEN HISTORICAL TRENDS IN DEVELOPMENT IN THIS AREA IT IS LIKELY THAT THE '50%' REFERENCE MAPS WILL ACCURATELY REFLECT THE POSITION IN THIS AREA IN TEN YEARS TIME.

We are now giving you the opportunity to have some say in this matter.

A few points to bear in mind:

* The green space is predominantly farmland, either fenced or bordered by hedgerows.

* All existing footpaths will remain although they may, of course, cut through proposed developments.

* New developments will be serviced by adequate new roads etc leaving the flow of traffic at today's levels.

* All SSI's, listed buildings and ancient monuments will be safeguarded.

BACKGROUND INFORMATION

In a moment you will be shown a random selection of possible alternative development plans for this area. If you prefer the alternative to the relevant reference map, you will be asked how much you would be willing to pay to secure this alternative. If you do not prefer the alternative, you will simply be asked to state how much compensation you would require to put up with this alternative proposal.

A few points to bear in mind:

* You are allowed to return to any of the maps you are shown if you wish to change your answers.

* Whether you do or do not prefer any of the alternative plans you should always bear in mind any equivalent amenities elsewhere which would offer you similar opportunities.

* If you prefer an alternative you should state the *maximum* amount that you would be willing to pay for it bearing in mind all the other demands on your money.

* If you do not prefer an alternative and would require compensation to put up with it, you should state the *minimum* amount.

* Payments will be made to, or compensation paid from, an independent management company with charitable status.

* The answers you give will provide some indication of the general public's preferences for alternative proposals. Northavon Planning Department may make use of these indications.

VALUATION SECTION

12. 'Do you prefer the randomly selected map to the reference map shown?'

    2 = INDIFFERENT   1 = YES   0 = NO

    If 'YES' GO TO Q13

    If 'NO' GO TO Q14

    If 'INDIFFERENT' RECORD A VALUE OF ZERO AGAINST THE RANDOM MAP AND MOVE ON TO THE NEXT SELECTION

13. If 'YES' at Q12 above

    Repeat of relevant text from 'Background Information'

    You have indicated that you prefer this alternative proposal

    - What is the *maximum* amount you would be willing to pay on an annual basis to ensure this proposal is taken up rather than the proposal shown on the reference map? £___
    [RECORD VALUE AGAINST MAP NUMBER]

14. If 'no' at Q12 above

    Repeat relevant text from 'Background Information'
    You have indicated that you do not prefer this alternative proposal

    - What is the *minimum* compensation you would require on an annual basis to put up with this proposal rather than the proposal shown on the reference map?
    £___
    [RECORD VALUE AGAINST MAP NUMBER]

    [REPEAT FOR 15 ITERATIONS FROM Q12]

APPENDIX 3 - ADDITIONAL QUESTIONS

Respondent number _____

These questions are concerned with your experiences of any consultation exercises undertaken by local authority planners with regard to changes in land use or developments in your locality.

Please circle the correct response in each case.

EXHIBITIONS

Q1 Have you ever attended a public exhibition organised by the Local Authority Planning Department illustrating potential land use changes/ developments in your locality?

YES / NO If 'NO', go to Q4

Q2 If 'YES' to Q1, did you feel you had adequate opportunity to give comments?

YES / NO

Q3 If 'YES' to Q2, did you feel that your comments were recorded in a satisfactory way?

YES / NO

PUBLIC MEETINGS

Q4 Have you ever attended a public meeting (or public inquiry) organised by the Local Authority Planning Department illustrating potential land use changes/developments in your locality?

      YES / NO   If 'NO', go to Q7

Q5 If 'YES' to **Q4**, did you feel you had adequate opportunity to give comments?

      YES / NO

Q6 If 'YES' to **Q5**, did you fell that your comments were recorded in a satisfactory way?

      YES / NO

GENERAL

Q7 Other than at Exhibitions or Public Meetings, have you ever responded either verbally or in writing to the Local Authority Planning Department's proposals for developments in your locality?

      YES / NO

PLEASE ANSWER THIS QUESTION

Q8 This question requires you to consider your experience of the exercise you have just undertaken. In comparison to the traditional methods of gathering public opinion on planning issues (exhibitions, meetings, etc) do you consider that this approach - if taken to your home or place of work - would allow you to have a greater or lesser say in the development of Local Plans?

      MORE SAY   5   4   3   2   1   LESS SAY

Bibliography

Alty R and Darke R, 1987, 'A City Centre for People : Involving the Community in Planning for Sheffield's Central Area', *Planning Practice and Research*, vol 3, pp 7-12

Arnstein S, 1969, 'A ladder of citizen participation', *Journal of the American Institute of Planners*, 35, pp 216-224

Arrow K J, 1951, *Social Choice and Individual Values*, rev edn 1963, Wiley, New York

Arrow K J, 1986, 'Comments' in Cummings G *et al*, (eds), *Valuing Environmental Goods: A State of the Arts Assessment of the Contingent Method*, 1986, Rowman and Allanheld, Totowa, NJ

Arrow K, Solow R, Leamer E, Portney P, Randner R and Schuman H, 1993, 'Report of the NOAA Panel on Contingent Valuation', Federal Register, vol 58, no 10, January 15, pp 4601-4614

Bateman I J, Langford I H, Willis K G, Turner R K and Garrod G D, 1993, 'The Impacts of Changing Willingness to Pay Question Format in Contingent Valuation Studies: An Analysis of Open-Ended, Iterative Bidding and Dichotomous Choice Formats', CSERGE Working Paper GEC 93-05, University College London.

Bateman I, Turner R K and Bateman S, 1993, 'Extending Cost Benefit Analysis of UK Highway Proposals: Environmental Evaluation and Equity', *Project Appraisal*, vol 8, no 4, pp 213-224

Belson W A, 1968, 'Respondent Understanding of Survey Questions', *Polls*, vol 3, pp 1-13

Bergland O, Magnusson K and Navrud S, 1995, 'Benefit Transfer: Testing for Accuracy and Reliability', paper presented at the 6th Annual Conference of EAERE, Umea, Sweden, June 17-20

Bergstrom J C, 1990, 'Concepts and Measures of the Economic Value of Environmental Quality - A Review', *Journal of Environmental Management,* vol 31, no 3, pp 215-228

Bergstrom J C, Stoll J R and Randall A, 1990, 'The Impact of Information on Environmental Commodity Valuation Decisions', *American Journal of Agricultural Economics,* vol 72, no 3, pp 614-621

Birch E L, 1980, 'Radburn and the American Planning Movement', *Journal of the American Planning Association,* 46

Bishop R C and Heberlein T A, 1979, 'Measuring Values of Extra-Market Goods: Are Indirect Measures Biased?' *American Journal of Agricultural Economics,* vol 61, no 5, pp 926-930

Bishop R C and Herberlein T A, 1986, 'Does Contingent Valuation Work?' in Cummings G *et al*, (eds), *Valuing Environmental Goods,* 1986, Rowman and Allanheld, Totawa, N J

Bishop R C, Heberlein T A and Kealy M J, 1983, 'Hypothetical Bias in Contingent Valuation: Results from a Simulated Market', *Natural Resources Journal,* vol 23, no 3, pp 619-633

Blackman T, 1991a, ''People-Sensitive Planning': Communication, Property and Social Action', *Planning Practice and Research*, 6, (3), pp 11-15

Blackman T, 1991b, *Planning Belfast,* Avebury, Aldershot

Blowers A, 1993, *Planning for a Sustainable Environment: A Report to the Town and Country Planning Association*, Earthscan, London

Bohm P, 1972, 'Estimating Demand for Public Goods: An Experiment', *European Economic Review,* 3, pp 111-130

Bohm P, 1984, 'Revealing Demand for an Actual Public Good', *Journal of Public Economics,* vol 24, pp 135-151

Bowker J M and MacDonald H F, 1993, 'An Economic Analysis of Localized Pollution : Rendering Emissions in a Residential Setting', *Canadian Journal of Agricultural Economics*, vol 41, no 1, pp 45-49

Boyle K J and Bergstrom J C, 1992, 'Benefit Transfer Studies : Myths, Pragmatism and Idealism', *Water Resources Research*, vol 28, no 3, pp 657-663

Boyle K J, Welsh M P and Bishop R C, 1993, 'The Role of Question Order and Respondent Experience in Contingent Valuation Studies', *Journal of Environmental Economics and Management*, vol 25, no 1 part 2, pp S80-S99

Braden J B and Kolstad C D, 1991, (eds), *Measuring the Demand for Environmental Quality*, Elsevier, Amsterdam

Brennan G and Buchanan J, 1984, 'Voter Choice', *American Behavioural Scientist*, vol 28, no 2, pp 185-201

Brookshire D, 1992, 'Issues Regarding Benefits Transfer', paper presented at the 1992 Association of Environmental and Resource Economists Workshop, Snowbird, Utah, June 3-5

Brookshire D S, Eubanks L S and Sorg C F, 1986, 'Existence Values and Normative Economics: Implications for Valuing Water Resources', *Water Resources Research*, vol 22, no 11, pp 1509-1518

Brookshire D S, Ives B C and Schulze W D, 1976, 'The Valuation of Aesthetic Preferences', *Journal of Environmental Economics and Management,* vol 3, no 4, pp 325-346

Brookshire D S and Neill H R, 1992, 'Benefit Transfers: Conceptual and Empirical Issues', *Water Resources Research*, vol 28, no 3, pp 651-655

Brookshire D S, Randall A and Stoll J R, 1970, 'Valuing Increments and Decrements in Natural Resource Service Flows', *American Journal of Agricultural Economics,* vol 62, no 3, pp 478-488

Bruton M and Nicholson D, 1987, *Local Planning in Practice*, Hutchinson, London

Burke S, 1968, 'Citizen Participation Strategies', *Journal of the American Institute of Planners*, 34

Carson R T, 1991, 'Constructed Markets', in Braden J B and Kolstad C D (eds), *Measuring the Demand for Environmental Quality*, 1991, Elsevier, Amsterdam

Carson R T, Hanemann W M and Mitchell R C, 1986, 'Determining the Demand for Public Goods by Simulating Referendums at Different Tax Prices', manuscript, University of California, San Diego, in Mitchell and Carson, 1989, p 203

Carson R T, Mitchell R C, Hanemann W M, Kopp R J, Presser S and Ruud P A, 1992, *A Contingent Valuation Study of Lost Passive Use Values Resulting from the Exxon Valdez Oil Spill*, A Report to the Attorney General of the State of Alaska

Clarke E H, 1971, 'Multipart Pricing of Public Goods', *Public Choice*, vol II, pp 19-33

Clawson M, 1959, *Methods of Measuring the Demand for Outdoor Recreation*, Reprint No 10, Resources for the Future, Washington DC

Clawson M and Knetsch J, 1966, *Economics of Outdoor Recreation*, The Johns Hopkins University Press for Resources for the Future, Baltimore

Collins A and Evans A, 1993, 'Aircraft Noise and Residential Property Values: an Artificial Neural Network Approach', Discussion Paper no 26, March, Department of Economics, University of Portsmouth

Collins A, Newland P and Rhodes P, 1993, 'Applying 3-D Modelling, Interactive Media and Contingent Valuation to Understanding Cityscape Flux and Environmental Impact', Discussion Paper no 27, March, Department of Economics, University of Portsmouth

Collins A, Pitt M and Newland P, 1992, 'Reducing Potential Response Effect Biases in Contingent Valuation Studies: A Role for Interactive Multimedia Technology?' Discussion Paper no 22, January, Department of Economics, Portsmouth Polytechnic, (now University of Portsmouth)

Coursey D L, Hovis J and Schulze W D, 1987, 'The Disparity Between Willingness to Accept and Willingness to Pay Measures of Value', *Quarterly Journal of Economics*, vol 102, pp 679-690

Cummings R G, Brookshire D S and Schulze W D, 1986, (eds) *Valuing Environmental Goods: A State of the Arts Assessment of the Contingent Method*, Rowman and Allanheld, Totowa, N J

Dasgupta A K and Pearce D W, 1972, *Cost-Benefit Analysis: Theory and Practice*, the Macmillan Press, London

Davidoff P and Reiner T A, 1962, 'A choice theory of planning', *Journal of the American Institute of Planners*, 28

Davis J and O'Neill C, 1992, 'Discrete-Choice Valuation of Recreational Angling in Northern Ireland', *Journal of Agricultural Economics*, vol 43, no 3, pp 452-457

Deaton A and Muellbauer J, 1980, *Economics and Consumer Behaviour*, Cambridge University Press, New York

Domencich T A and McFadden D, 1975, *Urban Travel Demand. A Behavioural Analysis*, North-Holland, New York

Deck L B and Chestnut L G, 1992, 'Benefits Transfer: How Good is Good Enough?', paper presented at the 1992 Association of Environmental and Resource Economists Workshop, Snowbird, Utah, June 3-5

Department of the Environment, 1991, *Policy Appraisal and the Environment: A Guide for Government Departments*, HMSO, London

Department of the Environment, 1992, *Planning Policy Guidance Note 12; Development Plans and Regional Guidance*, HMSO, London

Desvousges W H, Dunford R W and Matthews K E, 1992a, 'Natural Resource Damages Valuation: Arthur Kill Oil Spill', paper presented at the 1992 Association of Environmental and Resource Economists Workshop, Snowbird, Utah, June 3-5

Desvousges W H, Naughton M C, and Parsons G R, 1992b, 'Benefit Transfer: Conceptual Problems in Estimating Water Quality Benefits Using Existing Studies', *Water Resources Research*, vol 28, no 3, pp 675-683

Desvousges W H, Smith V K and McGivney M P, 1983, 'A Comparison of Alternative Approaches for Estimating Recreation and Related Benefits of Water Quality Improvements', EPA-230-05-83-001, Washington DC, Office of Policy Analysis, US Environmental Protection Agency

Dickie M, Fisher A and Gerking S, 1987, 'Market Transactions and Hypothetical Demand Data: A Comparative Study', *Journal of the American Statistical Association*, 82, (397), pp 69-75

Drake L, 1992, 'The Non-Market Value of the Swedish Agricultural Landscape', *European Review of Agricultural Economics*, vol 19, no 3, pp 351-364

Dunleavy P, 1991, *Democracy, Bureaucracy and Public Choice*, Harvester Wheatsheaf, Hemel Hempstead

Dupuit J, 1844, 'On the Measurement of the Utility of Public Works', translated from the French in *International Economic Papers*, 1952, no 2, London

Evans R C and Harris R H D, 1982, 'A Bayesian Analysis of the Free Rider Meta Game', *Southern Economic Journal*, vol 49, pp 137-149

Fishbein M and I, 1975, *Belief, Attitude, Intention and Behaviour: An Introduction to Theory and Research*, Addison-Wesley, Reading, Mass

Fisher A C and Hanemann W M, 1990, 'Option Value: Theory and Measurement', *European Review of Agricultural Economics*, vol 17, no 2, pp 167-180

Freeman III A M, 1991, 'Factorial Survey Methods and Willingness-to-Pay for Housing Characteristics: A Comment', *Journal of Environmental Economics and Management*, vol 20, pp 92-96

Friedman M, 1953, *Essays in Positive Economics*, The University of Chicago Press

Friend J K and Hickling A, 1987, *Planning Under Pressure. The Strategic Choice Approach*, Pergamon Press, Oxford

Geddes P, 1915, *Cities in Evolution*, Norgate and Norgate, London

Godschalk D and Mills P, 1966, 'A Collaborative Approach to Planning Through Urban Activities', *Journal of the American Institute of Planners*, 32

Goodman A C, 1992, 'Measuring Willingness-to-Pay with Factorial Survey Methods: A Reply', *Journal of Environmental Economics and Management*, vol 22, pp 95-98

Goodman A C, 1989, 'Identifying Willingness-to-Pay for Heterogeneous Goods with Factorial Survey Methods', *Journal of Environmental Economics and Management*, vol 16, pp 58-79

Green C H and Tunstall S M, 1991, 'The Evaluation of River Water Quality Improvements by the Contingent Valuation Method', *Applied Economics*, vol 23, pp 1135-1146

Green J R and Laffont J-J, 1978, 'A Sampling Approach to the Free Rider Problem', in Sandmo A (ed) *Essays in Public Economics*, Lexington Books, Mass.

Green J R and Laffont J-J, 1979, *Incentives in Public Decision-Making*, North-Holland, New York

Groves T, 1973, 'Incentive in Teams', *Econometrica,* Vol 41, pp 617-631

Gujarati D, 1992, *Essentials of Econometrics*, McGraw-Hill, Singapore

Hammack J and Brown G M, 1974, *Waterfowl and Wetlands: Towards Bioeconomic Analysis*, The Johns Hopkins University Press for Resources for the Future, Baltimore

Hammond P J, 1991, 'Interpersonal Comparisons of Utility: Why and How They Are and Should Be Made', in Elster J and Roemer J E, (eds), 1991, *Interpersonal Comparisons of Well-Being*, Cambridge University Press, Cambridge

Hanemann M, 1986, *Willingness to Pay and Willingness to Accept: How Much Can They Differ?*, draft manuscript, Berkeley, Department of Agriculture and Resource Economics, University of California

Hanemann W M, 1991, 'Willingness to Pay and Willingness To Accept: How Much Can They Differ?', *The American Economic Review*, vol 81, no 3, pp 635-647

Hanley N and Munro A, 1991, 'Design Bias in Contingent Valuation Studies: the Impact of Information, Discussion Paper in Economics: 91/13, University of Sterling, UK, July

Hanley N D and Ruffell R J, 1993 'The Contingent Valuation of Forest Characteristics: Two Experiments', *Journal of Agricultural Economics*, vol 44, no 2, pp 218-229

Harrison G W, 1992, 'Valuing Public Goods with the Contingent Valuation Method: A Critique of Kahneman and Knetsch', *Journal of Environmental Economics and Management*, vol 23, no 3, pp 248-257

Harsanyi J C, 1953, 'Cardinal Utility in Welfare Economics and in the Theory of Risk-Taking', *Journal of Political Economy*, vol 61, pp 434-435

Harsanyi J C, 1955, 'Cardinal Welfare, Individualistic Ethics, and Interpersonal Comparisons of Utility', *Journal of Political Economy*, vol 63, pp 309-321

Hausman J A, 1993, (ed), *Contingent Valuation: A Critical Assessment*, Contributions to Economic Analysis series, vol 220, North-Holland, Amsterdam

Healey P and Gilroy R, 1990, 'Towards a People-Sensitive Planning', *Planning Practice and Research*, 5, (2), pp 21-29

Healey P, McNamara P, Elson M and Doak A, 1988, *Land Use Planning and the Mediation of Urban Change*, Cambridge University Press, Cambridge

Heberlein T A, 1986, 'Measuring Resource Values: The Reliability and Validity of Dichotomous Contingent Valuation Measures', paper presented at the American Sociological Association Meeting, New York, August

Hedges B M, 1976, *Community Preference Surveys in Structure Planning*, Social and Community Planning Research, London

Heintz H T, Hershaft A and Horak G C, 1976, *National Damages of Air and Water Pollution*, Enviro Control Inc, Rockville, Md

Hicks J R, 1941, 'The Rehabilitation of Consumer's Surplus', *Review of Economic Studies*, vol 8, pp 108-116

Hicks J R, 1943, 'The Four Consumer Surpluses', *Review of Economic Studies,* vol 11, pp 31-41

Hicks J R, 1956, *A Revision of Demand Theory*, Clarendon Press, Oxford

Hoehn J P, 1983, 'The Benefits-Costs Evaluation of Multi-Part Public Policy: A Theoretical Framework and Critique of Estimation Methods', PhD dissertation, University of Kentucky, in Mitchell and Carson, *Using Surveys to Value Public Goods: The Contingent Valuation Method*, 1989, Resources for the Future Washington DC

Hoehn J P and Loomis J B, 1993, 'Substitution Effects in the Valuation of Multiple Environmental Programs', *Journal of Environmental Economics and Management*, vol 25, no 1, part 1, pp 56-75

Hoehn J P and Randall A, 1982, 'Aggregation and Dissaggregation of Program Benefits in a Complex Policy Environment: A Theoretical Framework and Critique of Estimation Methods', paper presented at the American Agricultural Economics Association Summer meetings, Logan, Utah, in Mitchell and Carson, *Using Surveys to Value Public Goods: The Contingent Valuation Method*, 1989, Resources for the Future Washington DC

Hoehn J P and Randall A, 1989, 'Too Many Proposals Pass the Benefit Cost Test', *American Economic Review*, 79, pp 544-551

Houthakker H and Taylor L D, 1970, *Consumer Demand in the United States 1929-1970*, Harvard University Press, Cambridge, Mass

Hsiao C, 1986, *Analysis of Panel Data*, Cambridge University Press, New York

Hurwicz L, 1972, 'On Informationally Decentralized Systems', in McGuire C B and Radner R (eds), *Decision and Organisation: A Volume in Honor of Jacob Marschak*, North Holland, Amsterdam

Imber D, Stevenson G and Wilks L, 1991, *A Contingent Valuation Survey of the Kakadu Conservation Zone*, Australian Resource Assessment Commission, Research Paper No 3, AGPS, Canberra

Jacobs M, 1991, *The Green Economy*, Pluto Press, London

Jacobs M, 1996, 'Environmental Valuation, Deliberative Democracy and Public Decision-Making Institutions', in Foster J, (ed), forthcoming 1996, *Valuing Nature*, Routledge, London

Jackson J N, 1972, *The Urban Future*, Allen and Unwin, London

Jones F D, 1975, 'A Survey Technique to Measure Demand Under Various Pricing Strategies', *Journal of Marketing*, vol 39, no 3, pp 75-77

Jones-Lee M W, Hammerton M and Phillips R R, 1985, 'The Value of Safety: Results from a National Survey', *Economic Journal,* vol 95, pp 49-72

Kahneman D, 1986, 'Comments' in Cummings G *et al*, (eds), *Valuing Environmental Goods: A State of the Arts Assessment of the Contingent Method*, Rowman and Allanheld, Totowa, N J

Kahneman D and Knetsch J L, 1992a, 'Valuing Public Goods: The Purchase of Moral Satisfaction', *Journal of Environmental Economics and Management,* vol 22, pp 57-70

Kahneman D and Knetsch J L, 1992b, 'Contingent Valuation and the Value of Public Goods: A Reply', *Journal of Environmental Economics and Management*, vol 22, no 1, pp 90-94

Kahneman D and Tversky A, 1979, 'Prospect Theory: An Analysis of Decisions Under Risk', *Econometrica,* 47, (2), pp 263-291

Kanninen B J, 1993, 'Optimal Experimental Design for Double-Bounded Duhotomous Choice Contingent Valuation', *Land Economics*, vol 69, no 2, pp 138-146

Kealy M J, Montgomery M and Dovidio J F, 1990, 'Reliability and Predictive Validity of Contingent Values: Does the Nature of the Good Matter?', *Journal of Environmental Economics and Management*, vol 19, no 3, pp 244-263

Kealy M J and Turner R W, 1993, 'A Test of the Equality of Closed-Ended and Open-Ended Contingent Valuations', *American Journal of Agricultural Economics*, vol 75, no 2, pp 321-331

Kealy M J, Dovidio J F and Rockell M L, 1988, 'Accuracy in Valuation is a Matter of Degree', *Land Economics*, vol 64, no 2, pp 159-171

Knetsch J L, 1989, 'The Endowment Effect and Evidence of Nonreversible Indifference Curves', *The American Economic Review*, vol 79, no 5, pp 1277-1284

Knetsch J L, 1992, 'Preferences and Nonreversibility of Indifference Curves', *Journal of Economic Behavior and Organization*, vol 17, pp 131-139

Knetsch J L and Sinden J A, 1984, 'Willing to Pay and Compensation Demanded: Experimental Evidence of an Unexpected Disparity in Measures of Value', *Quarterly Journal of Economics*, vol 94, no 3, pp 507-521

Krutilla J V, 1967, 'Conservation Reconsidered', *American Economic Review,* vol 57, pp 787-796

Krutilla J V and Fisher A C, 1975, *The Economics of Natural Environments: Studies in the Valuation of Commodity and Amenity Resources*, The Johns Hopkins University Press for Resources for the Future, Baltimore

Kweit M and Kweit R, 1987, 'The Politics of Policy Analysis: The Role of Citizen Participation in Analytic Decision Making', in DeSario and Langton (eds), *Citizen Participation in Decision Making*, 1987, Greenwood Press, Westport, CT

Laffont J-J, 1979, (ed), *Aggregation and Revelation of Preferences*, North-Holland, New York

Lancaster K J, 1966, 'A New Approach to Consumer Theory', *Journal of Political Economy,* vol 74, no 2, pp 132-157

Langford I H, Bateman I J and Langford H D, 1994, 'A Multilevel Modelling Approach to Triple-Bounded Dichotomous Choice Contingent Valuation', paper presented at the annual meeting of EAERE, Dublin
Lardaro L, 1993, *Applied Econometrics*, Harper Collins, New York
Levin J and Nalebuff B, 1995, 'An Introduction to Vote-Counting Schemes', *Journal of Economic Perspectives*, vol 9, no 1, pp 3-26.
Lichfield N, 1964, 'Cost-Benefit Analysis in Plan Evaluation', *Town Planning Review*, vol 35, no 2, pp 159-169
Lichfield N, 1988, *Economics in Urban Conservation*, Cambridge University Press, Cambridge
Lichfield N, 1992, 'Making the Assessment Link', *Planning*, July, pp 4-5
Little I and Mirless J, 1974, *Project Appraisal and Planning for Developing Countries*, Heinemann, London
Loehman E T and De V H, 1982, 'Applications of Stochastic Choice Modelling to Policy Analysis of Public Goods: A Case Study of Air Quality Improvements', *Review of Economics and Statistics*, vol 64, no 3, pp 474-480
Loomis J B, 1989, 'Test-Retest Reliability of the Contingent Valuation Method: Comparison of General Population and Visitor Responses'. *American Journal of Agricultural Economics*, vol 711, no 1, pp 76-88
Loomis J B, Creel M and Park T, 1991, 'Comparing Benefit Estimates from Travel Cost and Contingent Valuation Using Confidence Intervals for Hicksian Welfare Measures', *Applied Economics*, vol 23, no 11, pp 1725-1731
Loomis J B, Lockwood M and DeLacey T, 'Some Empirical Evidence on Embedding Effects in Contingent Valuation of Forest Protection', *Journal of Environmental Economics and Management*, vol 25, no 1, part 1, pp 45-55
Lovell M C, 1983, 'Data Mining', *The Review of Economics and Statistics*, vol LXV, no 1, pp 1-12
Mäler Karl-Göran, 1974, *Environmental Economics: A Theoretical Inquiry*, The Johns Hopkins University Press for Resources for the Future, Baltimore
March J G and Simon H A, 1959, *Organisations*, Wiley, New York
Mariotti M, 1993, 'The Nash Solution and Independence of Revealed Irrelevant Alternatives', University of London, Queen Mary and Economics Dept, Paper no 293, (February)
Marshall A, 1920, *Principles of Economics*, 8th edition, Macmillan, London
Maxwell S, 1994, 'Valuation of Rural Environmental Improvements using Contingent Valuation Methodology: a Case Study of the Marston Vale Community Forest Project', *Journal of Environmental Management* 41, 385-399

McConnell K E, 1992, 'Model Building and Judgment: Implications for Benefit Transfers with Travel Cost Models', *Water Resources Research*, vol 28, no 3, pp 695-700

McDaniels T L, 1992, 'Reference Points, Loss Aversion and Contingent Values for Auto Safety', *Journal of Risk and Uncertainty*, vol 5, no 2, pp 187-200

McFadden D, 1974, 'Conditional Logit Analyses of Qualitative Choice Behaviour', in Zarembka P (ed) *Frontiers in Econometrics*, Academic Press, New York

McLoughlin J B, 1969, *Urban and Regional Planning - A Systems Approach*, Faber and Faber, London

McMillan J, 1979, 'Individual Incentives in the Supply of Public Inputs', *Journal of Public Economics*, vol 12, pp 87-98

Meyerson M and Banfield E G, 1955, *Politics, Planning and the Public Interest*, The Free Press, Glencoe

Mishan E J, 1970, 'What is Wrong with Roskill?', *Journal of Transport Economics and Policy*, vol 4, no 3, pp 221-234

Mishan E J, 1974, 'Flexibility and Consistency in Project Evaluation', *Economica*, February, pp 81-96

Mishan E J, 1981, *Economic Efficiency and Social Welfare*, Allen and Unwin, London

Mishan E J, 1982, 'The New Controversy about the Rationale of Economic Evaluation', *Journal of Economic Issues*, vol 16, no 1, pp 29-47

Mitchell R C and Carson R T, 1989, *Using Surveys to Value Public Goods: The Contingent Valuation Method*, Resources for the Future, Washington, DC

Morey E R, 1984, 'The Demand for Site-Specific Recreational Activities: A Characteristics Approach', *Journal of Environmental Economics and Management*, vol 8, no 4, pp 345-371

Mueller D C, 1989, *Public Choice II*, Cambridge University Press, New York

Muller J, 1992, 'From Survey to Strategy : Twentieth Century Developments in Western Planning Method', *Planning Perspectives*, vol 7, pp 125-155

Musser W W, Lampi K A, Musser L M and Obermiller F W, 1988, 'Test-Retest Reliability of Contingent Valuation Methods', paper presented at the annual meeting of the Northeast Agricultural and Resource Economics Association, in Reiling S D *et al*, 1990

Nash C, Pearce D W and Stanley J, 1975, 'An Evaluation of Cost Benefit Analysis Criteria', *Scottish Journal of Political Economy*, vol 22, no 2, pp 121-134

Nickerson C A E, 1993, 'Valuing Public Goods: A Comment on Harrison's Critique of Kahneman and Knetsch', *Journal of Environmental Economics and Management*, vol 25, no 2, pp 93-102

Norgaard R B, 1986, 'Environmental Evaluation Techniques and Optimisation in an Uncertain World', *Land Economics*, vol 62, no 2, pp 210-213

Northavon District Council, 1987, 'Bristol North Fringe Local Plan', Northavon District Council, Thornbury, Bristol

O'Doherty R, 1993, 'In Defence of Valuing Environmental Amenities', *Futures*, 25, (4), May, pp 465-467

O'Riordan, 1977, 'Citizen Participation in Practice : Some Dilemmas and Possible Solutions', in Sewell W R and Coppock J T (eds), *Public Participation in Planning*, 1977, John Wiley and Sons, London

Opaluch J J and Mazzotta M J, 1992, 'Fundamental Issues in Benefit Transfer and National Resource Damage Assessment', paper presented at the Association of Environmental and Resource Economists Workshop, Snowbird, Utah, June 3-5

Ozuna T, Jang K Y and Stoll J R, 1993, 'Testing for Misspecification in the Referendum Contingent Valuation Approach', *American Journal of Agricultural Economics*, vol 75, no 2, pp 332-338

Palmquist R B, 1991, 'Hedonic Methods', in Braden J B and Kolsted C D (eds), *Measuring the Demand for Environmental Quality*, 1991, Elsevier, Amsterdam

Pearce D W and Markandya A, 1989, *Environmental Policy Benefits: Monetary Valuation*, OECD, Paris

Pennington G, Topham N and Ward R, 1990, 'Aircraft Noise and Residential Property Values Adjacent to Manchester International Airport', *Journal of Transport Economics and Policy*, vol 25, (1), pp 49-59

Pessemier E A, 1960, 'An Experimental Method of Estimating Demand', *Journal of Business*, vol 33, pp 373-383

Poulton E C, 1977, 'Quantitative Subjective Assessments are Almost Always Biased, Sometimes Completely Misleading', *British Journal of Psychology*, vol 68, pp 409-425

Pratt J W, Wise D A and Zeckhauser R, 1979, 'Price Differences in Almost Competitive Markets', *The Quarterly Journal of Economics*, vol 93, pp 189-212

Rae D H, 1983, *The Value to Visitors of Improving Visibility at Mesa Verde and Great Smokey National Parks*, in Rowe R D and Chestnut L G, (eds), *Managing Air Quality and Scenic Resources at National Parks and Wilderness Areas*, 1983, Westview Press, CO

Randall A, 1986, 'The Possibility of Satisfactory Benefit Estimating with Contingent Markets', in Cummings G *et al*, (eds), *Valuing Environmental Goods: A State of the Arts Assessment of the Contingent Method*, Rowman and Allanheld, Totowa, N J

Randall A, 1991, 'Total and Nonuse Values', in Braden J B and Kolsted C D (eds), *Measuring the Demand for Environmental Quality*, 1991, Elsevier, Amsterdam

Randall A, Hoehn J P and Tolley G S, 1981, 'The Structure of Contingent Markets: Some Experimental Results', paper presented at the Annual Meeting of the American Economics Association, Washington, DC, December, in Mitchell and Carson, *Using Surveys to Value Public Goods: The Contingent Valuation Method*, 1989, Resources for the Future, Washington, DC

Randall A and Stoll J R, 1980, 'Consumer's Surplus in Commodity Space', *American Economic Review,* vol 70, no 3, pp 449-455

Rawls J, 1971, *A Theory of Justice*, Harvard University Press, Cambridge, Mass.

Reiling S D, Boyle K J, Phillips M L and Anderson M W, 1990, 'Temporal Reliability of Contingent Values', *Land Economics,* vol 66, no 2, pp 128-134

Roberts J, 1978, 'The Incentives for correct Revelation of Preferences and the Number of Consumers', in Sandmo A (ed) *Essays in Public Economics*, Lexington Books, Mass.

Rose R, 1989, *Ordinary People in Public Policy - A Behavioural Analysis*, Sage, London

Rosen S, 1974, 'Hedonic Prices and Implicit Markets: Product Differentiation in Pure Competition', *Journal of Political Economy*, vol 82, pp 34-35

Roskill Lord,1970, Commission on the Third London Airport, *papers on the proceedings: Stage III Research and Investigation - Assessment of Short-Listed Sites*, vol 17, parts 1 and 2, HMSO

Rossi P H and Nock S L, 1982, (eds), *Measuring Social Judgements: The Factorial Survey Approach*, Sage Publications, Beverley Hills

Rowe R D, d'Arge R C and Brookshire D S, 1980, 'An experiment on the Economic Value of Visibility', *Journal of Environmental Economics and Management,* vol 7, pp 1-9

Rowe R D and Chestnut L G, 1983, (eds), *Managing Air Quality and Scenic Resources at National Parks and Wilderness Areas*, Westview Press, CO

RTPI, 1982, *The Public and Planning : Means to Better Participation*, final Report of the Public Participation Working Party (Chair: John Dean) April, RTPI, London

Samuelson P, 1954, 'The Pure Theory of Public Expenditure', *Review of Economics and Statistics*, vol 36, pp 387-389

Schofield J, 1987, *Cost-Benedit Analysis in Urban and Regional Planning*, Unwin Hyman, London

Self P, 1993, *Government by the Market? The Politics of Public Choice*, MacMillan, Basingstoke

Sen A K, 1967, 'Isolation, Assurance and the Social Rate of Discount', *Quarterly Journal of Economics*, vol 81

Sen A K, 1995, 'Rationality and Social Choice', *American Economic Review*, vol 85, no 1, pp 1-24

Sewell W R D and Coppock J T, 1977, *Public Participation in Planning*, John Wiley and Sons, London

Shechter M, 1991, 'A Comparative Study of Environmental Amenity Valuations', *Environmental and Resource Economics*, vol 1, no 2, pp 129-155

Silverberg E, 1978, *The Structure of Economics: A Mathematical Analysis*, McGraw-Hill, New York

Simon H A, 1965, *Administrative Behaviour*, (revised edn), MacMillan, New York

Singh H, 1991, 'The Disparity Between Willingness to Pay and Compensation Demanded', *Economic Letters*, vol 35, no 3, pp 263-266

Skeffington A M, 1969, *People and Planning*, Report to the Ministry of Housing and Local Government, the Scottish Development Department and the Welsh Office, HMSO, London

Smith A G, Williams G and Houlder M, 1986, 'Community Influence on Local Planning Policy', *Progress in Planning*, vol 25, part 1

Smith V K, 1980, 'Experiments with a Decentralised Mechanism for Public Good Decisions', *American Economic Review*, vol 70, no 4, pp 584-599

Smith V K (ed), 1984, *Environmental Policy Under Reagan's Executive Order: The Role of Benefit-Cost Analysis*, University of North Carolina Press, Chapel Hill

Smith V K, 1991 'Household Production Functions and Environmental Benefit Estimation', in *Measuring the Demand for Environmental Quality* by Braden J B and Kolstad C D (eds), Elsevier, Amsterdam

Smith V K, 1992a 'On Separating Defensible Benefit Transfers From 'Smoke and Mirrors'', *Water Resources Research*, vol 28, no 3, pp 685-694

Smith V K, 1992b, 'Arbitrary Values, Good Causes and Premature Verdicts', *Journal of Environmental Economics and Management*, vol 22, no 1, pp 71-89

Smith V K and Huang J-C, 1993, 'Hedonic Models and Air Pollution: Twenty-Five Years and Counting', *Environmental and Resource Economics*, 3, pp 381-394

Smith V K and Huang J-C, 1995, 'Can Markets Value Air Quality? A Meta-Analysis of Hedonic Property Value Models', *Journal of Political Economy*, vol 103, no 1, pp 209-227

Smith V K and Kaoru Y, 1990, 'Signals or Noise: Explaining the Variation in Recreation Benefit Estimates', *American Journal of Agricultural Economics*, 72, (2), pp 419-433

Smith V K and Krutilla J V, 1982, 'Towards Reformulating the Role of Natural Resources in Economic Models', in Smith V K and Krutilla J V, (eds), *Explorations in Natural Resource Economics*, The Johns Hopkins University Press for Resources for the Future, Baltimore

Sorg C F and Loomis J B, 1984, 'Empirical Estimates of Amenity Forest Values: A Comparative Review', General Technical Report, RM-107, Rocky Mountain Forest and Range Experimental Station, Forest Services, US Department of Agriculture, Fort Collins, Colorado

South Yorkshire County Council, 1975, *Doncaster District Structure Plan Kit*, Barnsley: County Planning Officer

Sprecht S V, 1983, 'The Bureau of Land Management's Visual Resource Management System', in Rowe D and Chestnut L G, (eds), *Managing Air Quality and Scenic Resources at National Parks and Wilderness Areas*, Westview

Stevens T H, Echeverria J, Glass R J, Hager T and More T A, 1991, 'Measuring the Existence Value of Wildlife: What do CVM Estimates Really Show?' *Land Economics*, vol 67, no 4, pp 390-400

Stewart T R, 1983, *Visual Air Quality Values: Public Input and Informed Choice*, in Rowe R D and Chestnut L G, (eds), *Managing Air Quality and Scenic Resources at National Parks and Wilderness Areas*, 1983, Westview Press, CO

Sun H, Bergstrom J C and Dorfman J H, 1992, 'Estimating the Benefits of Groundwater Contamination Control', *Southern Journal of Agricultural Economics*, vol 24, no 2, pp 63-71

Thornley A, 1977, 'Theoretical Perspectives on Planning Participation', *Progress in Planning*, vol 7, part 1

Turner R K, 1988, (ed), *Sustainable Environmental Management: Principles and Practice*, Bellhaven, London (first edition)

Turner R K, 1993, (ed), *Sustainable Environmental Management: Principles and Practice*, Bellhaven, London (second edition)

Tversky A and Kahneman D, 1981, 'The Framing of Decisions and the Psychology of Choice', *Science*, 211, pp 453-458

Tybout A M and Zaltman G, 1974, 'Ethics in Marketing Research - Their Practical Relevance', *Journal of Marketing Research*, vol 11, pp 357-368

Tyne and Wear County Council, 1976, *Structure Plan: What's in it for us?*, Newcastle upon Tyne: Tyne and Wear County Council Director of Planning

Urga G, 1992, 'The Econometrics of Panel Data: A Selective Introduction', University of London, Queen Mary and Westfield College, Economics Dept, Paper no 282, (November).

Vining J and Orland B, 1989, 'The Video Advantage - A Comparison of Two Environmental Representation Techniques', *Journal of Environmental Management,* vol 29, pp 275-283

Walsh R G, Johnson D M and McKean J R, 1992, 'Benefit Transfer of Outdoor Recreation Demand Studies, 1968-1988', *Water Resources Research,* vol 28, no 3, pp 707-713

Watson J, 1991, 'Communication and Superior Co-operation in Two-Player Normal Form Games', *Economics Letters,* vol 35, no 3, pp 267-271

Webster B and Lavers A, 1991, 'The Effectiveness of Public Local Inquiries as a Vehicle for Public Participation in the Plan Making Process : A Case Study of the Barnet Unitary Development Plan Inquiry', *Journal of Planning and Environment Law,* pp 803-813

Whitehead J C, 1991, 'Environmental Interest Group Behaviour and Self-Selection Bias in Contingent Valuation Mail Surveys', *Growth and Change,* vol 22, no 1, pp 10-21

Whittington D, Smith V K, Okorafor A, Okore A, Liu J L and McPhail A, 1992, 'Giving Respondents Time to Think in Contingent Valuation Studies: A Developing Country Application', *Journal of Environmental Economics and Management,* vol 22, pp 205-225

Willig R D, 1976, 'Consumer Surplus Without Apology', *American Economic Review,* vol 66, no 4, pp 587-597

Willis K and Garrod G, 1991, 'Valuing Open Access Recreation on Inland Waterways: On-site Recreation Surveys and Selection Effects', *Regional Studies,* vol 25, no 6, pp 511-524

Willis K G, 1980, *The Economics of Town and Country Planning,* Granada, St Albans

Winpenny J T, 1991, *Values for the Environment. A Guide to Economic Appraisal,* HMSO, London

Wu P I, 1993, 'Substitution and Complementarity in Commodity Space: Benefit Evaluation of Multidimensional Environmental Policy', *Academia Economic Papers,* vol 21, no 1, pp 151-182

Index

ACORN 110, 111, 127, 129, 133, 142
aggregation v, 2, 5, 8, 9, 165, 166
Alty and Darke 21-23, 25, 136
Arnstein 21-23, 136, 159
Arrow v, 1-6, 8, 9, 30, 32, 35, 40, 76, 87, 93, 104, 107, 108, 137, 149, 159
Arrow et al. 1, 87, 107, 108

Bateman et al. 36, 108
Belson 84, 159
benefit transfer (BT) vi, ix, xiii, xiv, 14, 33, 36, 37, 42, 46, 64-70, 72-75, 93, 95, 105, 109, 110-112, 125, 128, 132, 135, 138-140, 159, 160, 162, 169, 173
Bergland et al. 74, 128, 140
Bergstrom et al. 83, 84
Birch 19, 160
Bishop and Heberlein 51, 60, 81, 87, 108
Bishop et al. 81
Bishop, Heberlein and Kealy 51
Blackman 21, 24, 25, 136, 160
Blowers et al. 13
Bohm 60, 79, 81, 160
Bowker and MacDonald 111, 120
Boyle and Bergstrom 66, 69, 73

Boyle et al. 59
Breheny and Batey 19
Brennan and Buchanan 8
Brookshire 39, 61, 66, 68, 70, 74, 76, 79, 115, 160-162, 170
Brookshire and Neill 66, 68
Brookshire et al. 39, 79, 115
Bruton and Nicholson 23
Burke 21, 161

Carson 8, 37-40, 44, 51, 52, 76-84, 86, 161, 165, 168, 170
Carson et al. 40
Clarke 80, 161
Clawson 11, 43, 161
Clawson and Knetsch 43
Collins and Evans 111
Collins et al. 84, 86, 133
Community Technical Aid 24, 136, 137
contingent valuation (CVM) v-viii, xiii, xiv, 1, 2, 5, 7, 8, 10, 12-14, 17, 31, 32, 33, 35, 36, 39, 40, 42-44, 46, 47, 50-52, 54, 56, 57, 59, 60-65, 72-83, 85, 87-89, 92-94, 95, 96, 99, 101, 104-107, 110-112, 115, 128, 132, 135, 138-142, 159-161, 163-170, 172, 173
Coursey et al. 52

Cummings et al. 64
Cummings, Brookshire and Schulze 61

Dasgupta and Pearce 3, 13, 137
Davidoff and Reiner 20, 33
Davis and O'Neill 59
Deck and Chestnut 68
Desvousges et al. 67-69, 87, 109
Dickie et al. 60
DoE 13, 23
Drake 111, 162
Dupuit 9, 163

embedding 2, 40-42, 82, 139, 167
Evans and Harris 80
existence value 38-40, 51, 52, 172

factorial survey design vi, 14, 74, 75, 95, 99, 104-106, 138, 139, 141
Fishbein and Ajzen 58, 59, 82, 107
Fishbein-Ajzen ix, 57, 58, 60, 63, 107, 131
Fisher and Hanemann 38
Freeman 95, 100, 101, 163
Friend and Hickling 18, 20
functional form 8, 44, 45, 72, 73, 89, 98, 119, 120, 126

Geddes 18, 19, 163
Godschalk and Mills 21
Goodman 95, 98-101, 163
Green and Lafont 80
Green and Tunstall 38, 39, 86, 87, 91
Groves 80, 163
Gujarati 112, 163

Hammack and Brown 51
Hammond 7, 9, 164
Hanemann 38, 50, 51, 161, 163, 164
Hanley and Munro 83

Hanley and Ruffell 37, 73, 96
Harrison 42, 164, 169
Harsanyi 7, 164
Healey 19, 21, 22, 24, 164
Healey and Gilroy 21, 22, 24
Hedges 23, 164
hedonic pricing 11, 14, 35, 36, 43-47, 61, 99, 101, 139
Hoehn 40-42, 52, 165, 170
Hoehn and Loomis 41
Hoehn and Randall 40, 42, 52
Houthakker and Taylor 51

interpersonal comparisons 1, 3-6, 9, 137
Imber et al. 115

Jacobs 7, 8, 132, 137, 165
Jones-Lee et al. 63

Kahneman and Knetsch 40-42, 56, 164, 169
Kahneman and Tversky 52
Kanninen 88, 166
Kealy and Turner 87, 88
Kealy et al. 59-61
Knetsch 40-43, 51, 53, 54, 56, 119, 161, 164, 166, 169
Knetsch and Sinden 51
Krutilla 37-39, 166, 172
Krutilla and Fisher 38, 39
Kweit and Kweit 6, 23, 25, 33

Lancaster 14, 96, 139, 166
Langford et al. 88
Levin and Nalebuff 2, 4, 137
Lichfield 24, 96, 167
Little and Mirlees 6
Loehman and De 63
Loomis et al. 41, 61

Marshall 9, 167
Maxwell 113, 167

McConnell 67, 168
McDaniels 54, 168
McLoughlin 19, 20, 168
McMillan 80, 168
measurement error 110, 119, 126
meta-analysis 45, 72, 75, 172
mis-specification bias 126, 128
Mishan 6, 11, 168
Mitchell and Carson 8, 37-39, 44, 51, 52, 76-81, 83, 84, 161, 165, 170
Mueller 3-5, 30, 168
Muller 18-20, 168
Musser et al. 63

Nash, Pearce and Stanley 6
Nickerson 42, 169
Norgaard 23, 169

O'Doherty 61, 169
O'Riordan 32, 169
omitted variable 126, 127
Opaluch and Mazzotta 66
option value 38, 39, 163
Ozuna et al. 88

Palmquist 44, 169
participation v, vi, vii, ix, xiii, 1, 4, 9-14, 17, 18, 21-27, 31-37, 43, 45, 46, 74, 75, 82, 93, 95, 103, 104, 131, 132, 135-138, 140, 141, 142, 143, 147, 159, 161, 166, 169-173
payment mechanism 59, 60, 76, 106-108, 116
Pennington et al. 111
Poulton 87, 169
Pratt, Wise and Zeckhauser 57
quasi-option value 38, 39

Rae 100, 169
Randall 33, 38, 40, 42, 43, 46, 50-52, 76, 160, 161, 165, 170

Randall and Stoll 50, 51
Randall, Hoehn and Tolley 40
Rawls 7, 170
Reiling et al. 63, 65, 74
reliability vi, ix, 36, 54, 56, 59, 63-65, 67, 68, 74, 76, 80, 82, 93, 107, 108, 115, 139, 159, 164, 166-168, 170
Rosen 11, 44, 170
Roskill 11, 168, 170
Rossi and Nock 97-99
Rowe et al. 79
Rowe, d'Arge and Brookshire 76

sample size 70, 75, 76, 79, 80, 99, 108, 112, 119, 126-128, 140-142
Schofield 24, 171
Sen 2, 3, 7, 51, 137, 171
Sewell and Coppock 21
Shechter 61, 62, 171
Simon ix, 19, 167, 171
Singh 52, 171
Skeffington Report 17, 22, 135, 136
Smith 42, 45, 57, 61, 62, 67, 69, 72, 73, 79, 162, 171-173
Smith and Huang 45, 72
Smith and Kaoru 72
socio-economic characteristics 72, 73, 75, 99, 100, 109-111, 126, 128, 129, 133
Sorg and Loomis 42, 66, 70
South Yorkshire County Council 4, 172
starting point bias 54, 56, 87
Stevens et al. 39
Stewart 96-98, 138, 172
strategic behaviour viii, 4, 5, 13, 32, 35, 46, 56, 77-80, 83, 88, 93, 94, 107, 112, 140
Sun et al. 38

Thornley 21, 172
total economic value vi, 12, 14, 35-37, 43, 45, 51, 52, 60, 61, 82, 85, 99
travel cost viii, 8, 11, 14, 35, 36, 43-47, 61, 73, 139, 167, 168
Turner 13, 51, 87, 88, 159, 166, 172
Tversky and Kahneman 52
Tybout and Zaltman 88, 92
Tyne and Wear County Council 5, 173

validity vi, ix, 36, 43, 54, 56, 57, 59-61, 63, 64, 66-68, 76, 81, 82, 89, 92, 93, 106, 139, 164, 166

vicarious use value 38, 40
Vining and Orland 84

Walsh et al. 66, 70, 72, 110
Watson 80, 173
Webster and Lavers 17, 21, 23-25, 136
weighting 4, 6-8, 20, 21, 26, 28, 30, 32, 104
Whitehead 80, 173
Whittington et al. 107
Willig 50, 51, 173
Willis xi, 3-5, 37, 43, 159, 173
Willis and Garrod 37, 43
Wu 41, 173